Cambridge Elements ≡

Elements in Campaigns and Elections
edited by
R. Michael Alvarez
California Institute of Technology
Emily Beaulieu Bacchus
University of Kentucky
Charles Stewart III
Massachusetts Institute of Technology

ELECTIONS AND SATISFACTION WITH DEMOCRACY

Citizens, Processes, and Outcomes

Jean-François Daoust
Université de Sherbrooke

Richard Nadeau
Université de Montréal

CAMBRIDGE
UNIVERSITY PRESS

CAMBRIDGE
UNIVERSITY PRESS

Shaftesbury Road, Cambridge CB2 8EA, United Kingdom

One Liberty Plaza, 20th Floor, New York, NY 10006, USA

477 Williamstown Road, Port Melbourne, VIC 3207, Australia

314–321, 3rd Floor, Plot 3, Splendor Forum, Jasola District Centre,
New Delhi – 110025, India

103 Penang Road, #05–06/07, Visioncrest Commercial, Singapore 238467

Cambridge University Press is part of Cambridge University Press & Assessment,
a department of the University of Cambridge.

We share the University's mission to contribute to society through the pursuit of
education, learning and research at the highest international levels of excellence.

www.cambridge.org
Information on this title: www.cambridge.org/9781009454469

DOI: 10.1017/9781009128032

First published 2023

A catalogue record for this publication is available from the British Library

ISBN 978-1-009-45446-9 Hardback
ISBN 978-1-009-12428-7 Paperback
ISSN 2633-0970 (online)
ISSN 2633-0962 (print)

Additional resources for this publication at www.cambridge.org/9781009454469

Elections and Satisfaction with Democracy

Citizens, Processes and Outcomes

Elements in Campaigns and Elections

DOI: 10.1017/9781009128032
First published online: September 2023

Jean-François Daoust
Université de Sherbrooke

Richard Nadeau
Université de Montréal

Author for correspondence: Jean-François Daoust, jf.daoust@usherbrooke.ca

Abstract. Satisfaction with democracy is a vastly studied research topic. While scholars know ample key factors directly affecting citizens' satisfaction with democracy, much less is known about how context shapes these relationships. This Element aims to make sense of this context by showing that elections (electoral processes and outcomes) influence citizens' satisfaction with democracy in different ways according to the quality of a democratic regime. To do so, it leverages the datasets from the Comparative Study on Electoral Systems and argues that social scientists must take advantage of the increased availability of rich comparative datasets. These analyses lead the authors to conclude that elections do not only have different impacts on citizens' satisfaction with democracy based on the quality of the democratic regime that they live in but that the nature of the meaning attributed to electoral processes and outcomes varies between emergent and established democracies.

Keywords: satisfaction with democracy, elections, political behaviour, winner–loser gap, Losers' consent

ISBNs: 9781009454469 (HB), 9781009124287 (PB), 9781009128032 (OC)
ISSNs: 2633-0970 (online), 2633-0962 (print)

Contents

An online appendix is available at Cambridge.org/Daoust

1 Elections and Satisfaction with Democracy: Introduction

1.1 Introduction

Satisfaction with democracy (SWD) is a vastly studied topic in social sciences. Political scientists, sociologists, psychologists, economists, and scholars in communication have all conducted extensive research on this question. As we write this introduction, a basic search on Google Scholar for satisfaction with democracy yields approximately 1,550,000 general results, and more than 10,500 outcomes when looking for the exact expression.[1] There are both normative and empirical reasons for why researchers are interested in better understanding citizens' satisfaction with the functioning of their democratic institutions. The vast majority of people and many theorists believe that liberal democratic regimes offer the best set of principles and mechanisms to keep elected officials accountable to citizens and responsive to their demands (Estlund 2007; Sen 1999; Singer 1973; Waldron 1999). The extent to which citizens are satisfied with their political institutions represents an important indicator of a healthy democratic culture. Hence, deepening our knowledge of citizens' assessments of their political institutions is crucial, even more so because they seem to have become more critical of these institutions over time (Dalton 2004; Inglehart 1999; Norris 1999, 2011). Moreover, several researches suggest that a minimum level of satisfaction with the performance of democratic institutions represents a key condition for ensuring the emergence, consolidation, and stability of democratic regimes (Bernauer and Vatter 2011; Easton 1965; Lipset 1959).

Democracy consists of a set of principles and rules that allow for peaceful decision-making (Dahl 1989; Lipset 1959; Nadeau and Blais 1993; Norris 2019). Evaluating the impact of the electoral processes and outcomes on citizens' attitudes is crucial to understanding citizens' assessments of how their democratic institutions work in practice (Bernauer and Vatter 2011; Easton 1965; Harteveld 2021; Linde and Ekman 2003). In this sense, every election represents both a test for democracy and a potential threat to its regime support (Dennis 1970; Ginsberg and Weissberg 1978; Schattschneider 1960). While this is clearly the case for hybrid or autocratic political regimes, we believe that, to a certain extent, it is applicable to any regime, including well-established ones – the 2020 US presidential election and its aftermath being a telling example. The electoral process and citizens' perceptions of this process (e.g., whether it is fair, generates responsive governments, etc.) become particularly important, given that they themselves may play a substantial role in reinforcing (or weakening) people's

---

[1] A search restricted to Web of Science including "satisfaction with democracy" or "democratic satisfaction" returns more than 2,500 articles (Valgarðsson and Devine 2021: note 1).

views about the democratic system in which they live in (Birch 2008; Ginsberg 1982; Nadeau et al. 2000; Norris 2019).

The preceding lines suggest that citizens' support for democracy can be conceived of as a combination of citizens' diffuse support for democratic principles and of a running tally formed of continuous assessments of the (more contextual) performance of democratic institutions. From this perspective, SWD represents a "summary index," which can vary over time, because citizens' evaluations keep being added to this "total" as a result of their continuous and cumulative assessments of the basket of desirable political and economic goods produced by the system (Huang et al. 2008; Linz and Stepan 1996a, 1996b). This conceptualization is neatly encapsulated by Evans and Whitefield (1995: 503) who claim that: "people support democracies because they are seen to work, reflecting respondents' experience of the pay-offs from democracy itself."

Satisfaction with democracy thus appears to be a key indicator of democratic regimes' vitality. Since free and competitive elections form the cornerstone of democratic systems (Dahl 1971, 1989; Linz and Stepan 1996a; Przeworski 1991), it is crucial to examine the links between various aspects of the electoral process and citizens' level of satisfaction with democracy. Hence, it is unsurprising that a lot of research has been conducted to study these links. For instance, there is an important body of literature relating citizens' electoral status (winners, losers, or abstainers) with their level of SWD (Anderson et al. 2005; Dahlberg and Linde 2016; Hooghe and Stiers 2016; Nadeau and Blais 1993). Scholars have also paid a great deal of attention to the connection between voting systems and SWD (Aarts and Thomassen 2008; Anderson and Guillory 1997; Marien and Kern 2018; Singh et al. 2012). Another important strand of work has examined attitudes in emergent and established democracies in order to determine whether the impact of perceptions and expectations about the electoral process on citizens' level of SWD may vary across space and time (Dahlberg et al. 2015; Nadeau et al. 2021; Norris 2011; Powell 2004; Reher 2015).

Despite the abundant work aiming to explain citizens' levels of satisfaction with democracy, the literature on the role of elections and the electoral process still suffers from several important gaps. For example, numerous studies have examined the conditions under which the conduct of elections is likely to either engender public confidence or to lead citizens to question the fairness of the electoral process (Birch 2008; Norris 2017, 2019). There exists, however, scant research on the relationship between citizens' perceptions of electoral fairness and SWD, and little work has analyzed the links between instances of electoral fraud, contestation, and citizens' assessments of their democratic institutions

(Alvarez et al. 2020; Daxecker et al. 2019; Fortin-Rittberger et al. 2017; Moehler 2009; Norris 2019). Moreover, to date, no systematic studies have been conducted on the relationship between the role of third-party actors and, most notably, the presence of international observers to ensure the integrity of the electoral process and SWD (Birch 2008, 2011; Hyde and Marinov 2012, 2014; Chernykh and Slovik 2015).

Important connections between the electoral process and satisfaction with democracy are yet to be fully explored, and the same can be said about the impact of electoral outcomes on SWD. Although research suggests that citizens' assessments of electoral institutions are more *output-related* (i.e., heavily shaped by whether one ends up on the winning or the losing side) in emergent democracies and more *process-oriented* (i.e., mostly influenced by citizens' sense that their participation matters to the political process; see Dahlberg et al. 2015; Kittilson and Anderson 2011; Lührmann et al. 2017; Reher 2015) in established democracies, the existence of this relationship has not been tested in a systematic fashion so far. Furthermore, the assumption that the relative impact of citizens' perceptions about electoral responsiveness on their level of SWD may be context-dependent is also not clearly established in the current literature. Finally, although the emergence of a "winner–loser gap" in post-electoral citizens' level of SWD is one the most robust relationships in political science (i.e., winners are systematically more satisfied with democracy), we still know very little about what factors generate this gap. Is it winners who are benefiting from a boost? Is it that losers are becoming more negative? Is it due to both? And, why? We do not know much about these important questions. Finally, we have little cues about the impact of electoral outcomes for situations that are quite frequent but very much overlooked in the literature, for example when some voters support the most popular party (in terms of vote shares) but end up in the opposition and excluded from the government. This context, characterized as "electoral inversions" or "reversed legitimacy," might have important implications for citizens' satisfaction with democracy.

The gaps described above justify undertaking a systematic effort to better understand the key relationships affecting citizens' evaluations of their political institutions. We aim to contribute to this research strand with this Element. We also believe that the datasets recently made available through major international collaborations and used throughout our work represent an important added value for the general interest of this Element.

Most of the relevant literature about the relationship between elections and SWD is based on data that are quite limited across time and space. Therefore, many studies focusing on macro-level factors do not benefit from substantial variance at their level of interest (e.g., quality of democracy, economic growth, etc.). The robustness and the generalizability of these findings are therefore quite limited. To carry out various analyses, we leverage data from the Comparative Study of Electoral Systems (CSES) project. The full datasets include more than 350,000 respondents, covering 207 elections across 56 countries between 1996 and 2020. A crucial advantage of this dataset is that, even when we cannot use every module for every test, it still offers an interesting deal of variance on macro-level features (more than what is usually found in previous studies). Overall, our approach, which we now turn to, relies on this dataset and offers one of the most extensive assessments of the key contextual factors related to elections and how they shape citizens' satisfaction with democracy.

1.2 Our Approach

Inspired by the pioneering work of Easton (1965, 1975), two broad types of political support have been identified. On the one hand, *diffuse support* represents a long-standing predisposition that "refers to evaluations of what an object is or represents – the general meaning it has for a person – not what it does" (Easton 1965: 273). On the other hand, *specific support* is based on citizens' evaluations of a system's performance in providing desirable outputs as a whole. Researchers usually acknowledge this difference and stress the importance of carefully specifying whether a work's main goal is to analyze citizens' support for democratic principles (i.e., diffuse support) or to better understand how they evaluate the performance of democratic regimes (i.e., specific support). Our research deals with specific support, with a focus on its most used measure, that is, SWD.

Previous work on SWD can be divided into two main strands of literature. First, microlevel research, which focuses on the individual characteristics of satisfied and dissatisfied citizens. The main goal of this type of work is to better understand: (1) sociodemographic factors (Anderson et al. 2005; Foa et al. 2020), (2) opinions, attitudes, and values (Kornberg and Clarke 1994; Magalhães 2016), or (3) political behaviors (Han and Chang 2016; Kostelka and Blais 2018) linked to individuals' levels of satisfaction with democracy. Macro-level research, for its part, focuses on (1) the direct effect of key national macro-level variables, such as economic performance, type of electoral systems, and the quality of democracy (Dassonneville and McAllister 2020; Marien and Kern 2018), as well as (2) the moderating effect of these variables on individual-level determinants of satisfaction with democracy (Anderson and Guillory 1997; Rohrschneider and Loveless 2010). Our contribution is in this second, macro-level strand of research. More precisely, we make use of the

CSES to integrate context and clarify the conditions related to the electoral process under which determinants of satisfaction with democracy become more or less important.

Our main objective is to provide the first systematic account of how context shapes the kind of determinants that are key in making sense of citizens' satisfaction with democracy. To do so, we capitalize on the unique datasets of the CSES to achieve this goal, and more precisely, we leverage the five modules of the CSES (2015a, 2015b, 2015c, 2018, and 2021) to assemble a large comparative dataset. The features that make the CSES data particularly suitable for a systematic analysis of the contextual determinants of satisfaction with democracy include:

- The breadth of its geographical coverage (fifty-seven countries).
- The importance of the elections (i.e., national) analyzed in each country.
- The time span of the data collection (from 1996 to 2020).
- The timing of the fieldwork (i.e., most of the data are collected shortly after the election).[2]
- The large number of elections (207).
- The substantial variance on key macro-level variables (quality of democracy, etc.).
- The quality and comparability of the survey (e.g., same question wording).
- The large number of respondents surveyed (more than 350,000).

Most electoral inquiries included in the CSES comprise more than 1,000 respondents, usually forming a nationally representative sample (based on different variables, including age, gender, and education).[3] Table 1 summarizes the number of unique countries, elections, and respondents per module. It also details which elections specifically were included. Not surprisingly, however, some data are missing, which prevents us from systematically including every single election of the CSES. Luckily, there are very few. Table A1 of the Online Appendix shows which elections were excluded as well as the justification (i.e., the variables that were missing). For example, satisfaction with democracy was not part of the national study's questionnaire in four elections (out of 207), which are Chile in 1999 and 2009, Peru in 2000, and Argentina in 2015.

Other limits should be noted. First, there is some variance in the mode of data collection. While most respondents answered the questionnaire through an in-person interview, several national teams contacted people via telephone, a

---

[2] Most election studies are on the field few days after the election, and about 80 percent of the respondents answered the questionnaire within the first two months following the election day.

[3] For more information on specific election-year samples, see the publicly available codebook from the CSES (2015a, 2015b, 2015c, 2018, and 2021).

Table 1 Elections included in the CSES

	Module 1 (1996–2001)	Module 2 (2001–2006)	Module 3 (2006–2011)	Module 4 (2011–2016)	Module 5 (2016–2020)
Albania		2005			
Argentina				2015	
Australia	1996	2004	2007	2013	2019
Austria			2008	2013	2017
Belarus	2001		2008		
Belgium	1999, 1999	2003			2019, 2019
Brazil		2002	2006, 2010	2014	
Bulgaria		2001		2014	
Canada	1997	2004	2008	2011, 2015	2019
Chile	1999	2005	2009		2018
Costa Rica					2018
Croatia			2007		
Czech Republic	1996	2002	2006, 2010	2013	
Denmark	1998	2001	2007		2019
Estonia				2011	
Finland		2003	2007, 2011	2015	2019
France		2002	2007	2012	2017
Germany	1998	2002, 2002	2005, 2009	2013	2017
Great Britain	1997	2005		2015	2017
Greece			2009	2012, 2015	2015
Hong Kong	1998, 2000	2004	2008	2012	2016
Hungary	1998	2002			2018
Iceland	1999	2003	2007, 2009	2013	2016, 2017
Ireland		2002	2007	2011	2016
Israel	1996	2003	2006	2013	2020
Italy		2006			2018
Japan	1996	2004	2007	2013	
Kenya				2013	
Kyrgyzstan		2005			
Latvia			2010	2011, 2014	
Lithuania	1997				2016
Mexico	1997, 2000	2003	2006, 2009	2012, 2015	
Montenegro				2012	2016
Netherlands	1998	2002	2006, 2010		2017
New Zealand	1996	2002	2008	2011, 2014	2017, 2020
Norway	1997	2001	2005, 2009	2013	2017
Peru	2000, 2001	2006	2011	2016	
Philippines		2004	2010	2016	
Poland	1997	2001	2005, 2007	2011	
Portugal	2002	2002, 2005	2009	2015	2019
Romania	1996	2004	2009	2012, 2014	

Table 1 (cont.)

	Module 1 (1996–2001)	Module 2 (2001–2006)	Module 3 (2006–2011)	Module 4 (2011–2016)	Module 5 (2016–2020)
Russia	1999, 2000	2004			
Serbia				2012	
Slovakia			2010		2020
Slovenia	1996	2004	2008	2011	
South Africa			2009	2014	
South Korea	2000	2004	2008	2012	2016
Spain	1996, 2000	2004	2008		
Sweden	1998	2002	2006	2014	2018
Switzerland	1999	2003	2007	2011	2019
Taiwan	1996	2001, 2004	2008	2012	2016, 2020
Thailand	2001		2007	2011	2019
Tunisia					2019
Turkey			2011	2015	2018
Ukraine	1998				
United States	1996	2004	2008	2012	2016, 2020
Uruguay			2009		2019
Total	39 elections, 33 counties, $n =$ 62,409	41 elections, 38 counties, $n =$ 62,953	50 elections, 41 counties, $n =$ 80,163	45 elections, 39 counties, $n =$ 75,558	41 elections, 36 counties, $n =$ 76,123

Note: Belgium 1999 and Belgium 2019: two election studies were run in Belgium in 1999 – one in Belgium-Flanders and one in Belgium-Walloon. We combined them. Germany 2002: two election studies were run in Germany in 2002 – one was a telephone study and one was a mail-back study. We also combined them. Portugal 2002: the Portugal 2002 election study occurred during the transition between module 1 and module 2, so it is listed in both modules but only one is used.

self-administered online questionnaire, or a mix of methods. Research, however, does not suggest that the mode of data collection affects the inferences drawn by scholars (e.g., Dassonneville et al. 2020). Second, there can be issues regarding the translation within and across countries. Third, the number of observations is not homogenous across countries. Fourth, the meaning of some concepts included in the question wording may vary across contexts. One may think of the equivocal notion of "ideology," or perhaps "democracy" as in "satisfaction with democracy" – an issue that we address later in this section. We believe, however, that the merits of the CSES data outweigh the limitations and allow us to provide insightful analyses despite being drawn from imperfect data.

The CSES dataset will be supplemented with various macro-level data, including measures of economic development, income inequality, the electoral system, and, most importantly for our purposes, measures of the quality of democratic institutions and electoral processes, as well as information about the role of third-party actors, which includes international observers. These contextual indicators will be drawn from various sources, including the Varieties of Democracy (V-Dem) project (Coppedge et al. 2018), the World Bank (2019), Bormann and Golder's (2013) dataset political institutions across the world,[4] Solt's (2019) data on inequality, and Hyde and Marinov's (2012; 2019) National Elections Across Democracy and Autocracy Dataset (NELDA).

Satisfaction with democracy is the main dependent variable throughout this Element. It is measured with a single-item question that was included, as mentioned above, in the vast majority of election inquiries (203 out of 207). The question reads as follows: "On the whole, are you very satisfied, fairly satisfied, not very satisfied or not at all satisfied with the way democracy works in [name of the country]?" For the sake of simplicity and following many scholars (among others, see Anderson et al. 2005; Bol et al. 2018; Pfeifer and Schneck 2017), we use satisfaction with democracy as linear (rescaled from 0 to 1), which allows us to use mixed-effects linear regressions as our main estimation strategy.

Scholars have raised legitimate concerns about the validity of this widely used measure of SWD. More specifically, the comparability of the question has been at the core of many scholarly debates. There is a risk that survey respondents might interpret the question differently across countries, which might introduce a systematic bias and, thereby, prevent useful cross-national comparisons (Ananda and Bol 2020; Ariely 2015; Canache et al. 2001; Valgarðsson and Devine 2021). Uncovering the comparability of a question is not an easy task, but some researchers have nonetheless attempted to do so. For example, Ariely (2015) concluded from multiple-group confirmatory factor analyses that scholars can conduct valuable cross-national comparisons, yet the meaning of democracy might be different for a subsample of countries, that is, democracies of lower quality (measured using the Freedom House index). Previously, Dalton et al. (2007) raised this potential issue by asking whether "the average citizen – *especially in poor and less democratic nations* – can offer a reasonable definition of democracy" (p. 143, our emphasis). Using data from open-ended questions included in the World Values Survey, the authors not only concluded that most people have a common understanding of democracy, but that "previous thinking about citizens in developing nations has not done them justice" (Dalton et al. 2007: 153).

---

[4] We used the CSES' variable indicating which electoral formula was used in a given election, but Bormann and Golder's (2013) data were used to measure the electoral systems used in elections for which the CSES did not have information, that is, only five elections (from modules 1 and 2).

We can use the CSES to perform additional tests suggesting that our measure of satisfaction with democracy is comparable across contexts. We follow the approach proposed by Canache et al. (2001), who are among the most critical authors of this indicator. That is, we examine how variables linked to SWD vary from one country to another. The underlying rationale behind this is that, if satisfaction with democracy roughly measures the same concept across contexts, then we should expect that a set of meaningful variables will be systematically linked to this indicator across nations and that these observed relationships will be similar across space. Canache et al. (2001) make it clear that "[f]or instance, if SWD and system support are correlated in only 10 of the 17 Latinbarometer nations, this would be clear evidence that SWD represents different things in different places" (p. 522). The authors also mention that covariation is not enough: The magnitude of the correlations should be similar across countries. In other words, we should expect the correlation between a variable close to satisfaction with democracy to be systematically statistically significant across nations, and also of a similar magnitude. But what constitutes a "similar magnitude" is not obvious, and Canache et al. (2001: 522) "see it as reasonable that the correlations vary by less than 100 percent from one nation to another. In other words, we would see cause for concern in results indicating that the relationship between a variable tapping a certain type of political support and SWD is twice as strong in one nation as in another." We agree with the authors on both accounts.

Unfortunately, the CSES does not systematically include variables tapping various types of political support. However, module 2 includes a question measuring a more *diffuse* form of political support (compared to satisfaction with democracy), which asks respondents about democracy as the best political regime.[5] Moreover, modules 2 and 3 include a more *specific* form of political support (again, compared to satisfaction with democracy), asking respondents about their approval of their national government.[6] To evaluate whether these two variables systematically correlate with satisfaction with democracy and to compare the magnitude of their effects across countries, we predict satisfaction with democracy using these two variables separately (which is the most appropriate way in order to mimic Canache et al.'s approach). Online Appendix B provides descriptive statistics for the more diffuse and more specific political support variables, but it is worth mentioning that we use them as linear, ranging from a 0 to 1 scale. We ran an OLS

---

[5] The question was: "Please tell me how strongly you agree or disagree with the following statement: Democracy may have problems but it's better than any other form of government. Do you agree, strongly agree, disagree or disagree strongly with this statement?"

[6] The question was: "Now thinking about the performance of the government in [capital]/president in general, how good or bad a job do you think the government/president in [capital] has done over the past [number of years between the previous and the present election OR change in government.] years. Has it/he/she done a very good job? A good job? A bad job? A very bad job?"

regression predicting SWD in each country and plotted the thirty-six coefficients for the diffuse political support variable (from module 2) and forty-five coefficients for the more specific political support variable (from modules 2 and 3).[7] Figure 1 shows the findings.

We begin with the diffuse political support variable. First, all the thirty-six coefficients are in the same (positive) direction and statistically significant at $p < 0.05$ for the "democracy as the best regime" question (see Figure 1, left panel). This shows that our indicator of satisfaction with democracy fares very well with the first criterion outlined by Canache et al. (2001). The second criterion is about the magnitude of the effect. The mean effect is 0.169, meaning that we will consider values below 0.0845 or above 0.338 as substantially different. This range is illustrated by the dashed lines in Figure 1. There are two cases below the lower threshold of 0.08 (i.e., Canada and Spain), and none above the upper threshold. Hence, 34/36 (94.4 percent) of the estimates have a similar effect size. This is very reassuring.

Examining the correlations between the more specific political support question and SWD (Figure 1, right panel) leads to a similar conclusion.

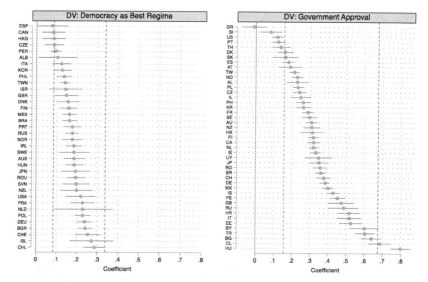

Figure 1 Different indicators of political support and their correlation with S

Note: Coefficients are plotted with 95 percent confidence intervals. The area between the dashed lines (vertical) represents the acceptable range of correlation as described in the text.

---

[7] In both cases, we include election fixed effects and also control for age, gender, education, and income as covariates in the regressions (e.g., Anderson et al. 2005: 20–21; Foa et al. 2020).

First, 44/45 coefficients are positive and statistically significant at $p < 0.05$, which (successfully) meets the first criterion of Canache et al. (2001). Second, the magnitude of the effect of a given coefficient would be substantially different if it is below 0.157 (half the mean) or 0.675 (twice the mean). Out of the forty-five coefficients, five are substantially weaker (GR, PT, SI, TH, US) and two are substantially greater (CL, HU). Hence, a total of thirty-eight out of the forty-five coefficients (86.6 percent of cases) display similar effects. Both sets of findings in Figure 1 are reassuring. First, SWD appears empirically distinct from the two different dependent variables tapping more diffuse and more specific political support. The average correlations are too low to claim that the questions tap the same concept. Second, these correlations are systematically in the same direction and the coefficients are of similar magnitudes, which suggests that the question used to tap SWD measures the same concept across contexts and is thus very likely comparable. Overall, we conclude that, despite fair critiques about the indicator of SWD, this widely used item offers an adequate and comparable measure of citizens' views about how democracy works *in practice* across national contexts (Linde and Ekman 2003: 391; Mattes and Bratton 2007: note 3).

Although the meaning does not seem to change substantially across contexts, the average levels of satisfaction with democracy might vary over time. After all, the CSES covers almost a quarter of a century, a period during which some have argued that citizens have become more distrustful of politics (Torcal 2014; Whiteley et al. 2016). Overall, the pooled dataset shows that most citizens are satisfied with the way democracy works and that the level is remarkably stable over time. First, Figure 2 shows the distribution of the variable. When recoded as linear, ranging from 0 to 1 as mentioned earlier, satisfaction with democracy displays a mean of. 0.52 and a standard deviation of 0.30. Second, Figure 3 shows the average value for SWD per election-year. It also includes a linear trend as well as a lowess regression. The patterns are very similar, and there is no evidence of nonlinearity. All in all, there is very little variation over time, suggesting that there is no long-term decline in satisfaction with democracy.

Moreover, external shocks, such as economic crises or the COVID-19 pandemic, could affect citizens' satisfaction with democracy. The most obvious economic shock across the time period is the 2008 financial crisis (Quaranta et al. 2021). However, as is clear from Figure 3, there is no detectable decrease after this shock. Moreover, the COVID-19 pandemic is definitely a major event with a potential to affect citizens' political support. The literature is, however, quite thin (but see Bol et al. 2020), and it will be interesting to see how this crisis will shape political support in the long run. The current CSES datasets, even with the most updated version from March 2022, included a very limited number of elections held in 2020. Israel, New Zealand, Slovakia, Taiwan, and the United States are the

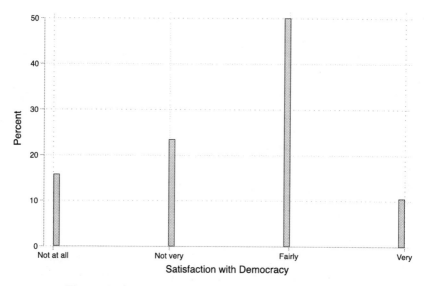

Figure 2 The distribution of satisfaction with democracy

Note: $N = 325{,}270$

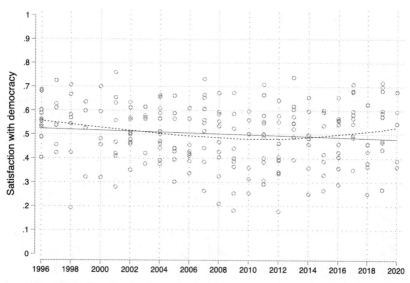

Figure 3 The distribution of satisfaction with democracy over time

Note: $N = 207$ (elections). Linear trends and local regression (using lowess command in Stata 16 with all options set at default) included.

only election studies conducted in 2020. Moreover, elections from Israel, Slovakia, and Taiwan were held very early in the year, before the World Health Organization officially declared COVID-19 a pandemic on March 11, 2020.

Overall, Figure 3 shows remarkable stability across twenty-four years. This stability can be quite surprising given the conventional wisdom that citizens are increasingly critical and distrustful when it comes to politics (Dalton 2004; Inglehart 1999; Norris 1999, 2011), and the belief that there is an increasing disconnect between citizens and democratic institutions (Foa and Mounk 2017). That said, the stability of satisfaction with democracy in the CSES data is in line with Anderson et al.'s (2021: 981), who recently concluded that

> [w]hile there are signs of democratic backsliding in specific countries, this has taken place within a broader context of stable global preferences for democratic government.

The stability of SWD shown in Figure 3 could be linked to the quality of the democracy of countries included in the CSES over time. Most democracies covered by the CSES are political regimes of high quality. As mentioned previously, we complement the CSES with V-Dem datasets. More precisely, we use the polyarchy variable (v2x_polyarchy), which measures the extent to which the ideal of electoral democracy is achieved in its fullest sense. This index is calculated by taking the average of both the weighted averages of the following indices: Freedom of association, clean elections, freedom of expression, elected officials, and suffrage, as well as the average of the five-way multiplicative interaction between these indices (see Coppedge et al. 2018).[8] This variable, which theoretically ranges from 0 to 1, has been used quite extensively to tap the quality of political regimes (e.g., Nadeau et al. 2021).

Figure 4 shows the distribution of the variable for countries included in the CSES. Overall, the mean of quality of democracy is 0.78 with a standard deviation of 0.17. There is still, however, a great deal of variance. For example, twenty-two elections were held in countries with a score of less than 0.5, and thirty-two can be found below 0.6. Moreover, although the CSES included a more diverse set of diversity over time (despite having a quite diverse pool in the very first module), the overall quality of democracy was very stable. Hence, we should not rule out the possibility that satisfaction with democracy is declining over time, but the lack of a downward trend in SWD (Figure 5) is likely not attributed to the quality of democracy surveyed in the CSES.

---

[8] See also the following from the codebook: "The electoral principle of democracy seeks to embody the core value of making rulers responsive to citizens, achieved through electoral competition for the electorate's approval under circumstances when suffrage is extensive; political and civil society organizations can operate freely; elections are clean and not marred by fraud or systematic irregularities; and elections affect the composition of the chief executive of the country. In between elections, there is freedom of expression and an independent media capable of presenting alternative views on matters of political relevance." (Coppedge et al. 2018: 43)

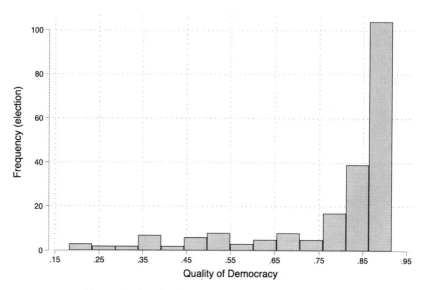

Figure 4 The distribution of quality of democracy

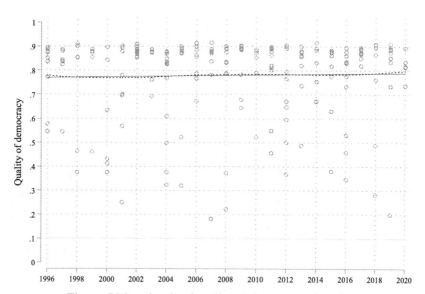

Figure 5 Mean levels of quality of democracy over time

Note: $N = 207$ (elections). Linear trends and local regression (using lowess command in Stata 16 with all options set at default) included.

1.3 Outline of the Element

The next three sections analyze citizens' satisfaction with democracy, by making sense of key contextual features that are either directly associated with SWD or moderate the impact of important variables determining citizens' SWD. In Section 2, we begin by examining citizens' perceptions of electoral fairness, which are central in explaining their SWD. We show that these perceptions are grounded in reality, that is, they are linked to the quality of a democracy, and that their impact on satisfaction with democracy is powerful. Perceptions of electoral fairness are, however, heavily shaped by the electoral status of voters (whether they voted for a winner or a loser), and this relationship is conditional on a country's quality of democracy. Finally, we analyze the impact of electoral monitoring. More precisely, we focus on the presence of international observers, which has never been used to understand citizens' SWD. Findings demonstrate that the presence of international observers can improve citizens' attitudes toward their democratic regime. However, this effect is only useful in low-quality contexts, compared to established democratic regimes where there is no such positive effect.

In Section 3, we capitalize on the distinction between *process-* and *output-* oriented (political) factors to explain how citizens' satisfaction with democracy varies across political regimes. The literature is clear about the importance of these variables, but we have a limited understanding of the conditions under which citizens will prioritize one criterion (related to the process or the output) over the other. In this section, we argue that we need to consider the quality of democracy to make sense of these relationships. The CSES allows us to provide the most extensive test of this kind, which shows that (1) the weight of process-related considerations in citizens' evaluation of how democracy works in their country increases as the quality of a democracy increases, and that (2) the weight of output-related considerations in citizens' evaluation of their political institutions decreases as the quality of a democracy increases.

In Section 4, we shed new light on the winner–loser gap in two ways. First, we establish more firmly that the quality of a democracy moderates the size of the winner–loser gap, and we show that this effect is due to both winners and losers, although their electoral status matters less in democracies of high quality. Second, we aim to disentangle different electoral statuses beyond the dichotomous view of being in or out of the government, by paying particular attention to contexts of "electoral inversions" – that is, when presidential candidates or parties benefit from the broadest support among citizens (i.e., vote share) but do not end up in government due to electoral rules. Again, the quality of a democracy in which these situations occur seems central to understanding the role of elections on citizens' SWD in contexts of disputed legitimacy.

In Section 5, we conclude by highlighting our contributions that focused on making sense of contextual relationships to better understand what shapes citizens' SWD. In this perspective, our results show that the role of elections on SWD may have a different meaning in established and emerging democracies. Our inquiry also restates the importance of large *N*-comparative datasets, such as CSES, for social science research, and that using them necessitates taking account of contexts. This becomes even more important as datasets are getting larger over time. Finally, we discuss the normative implications of our findings as well as ways of improving our understanding of elections and citizens' political support for future research.

2 Electoral Fairness, Electoral Monitoring, and Satisfaction with Democracy

2.1 Introduction

Free and competitive elections are the cornerstone of democratic systems and encapsulate the notion of electoral fairness (Dahl 1971, 1989; König et al. 2022; Linz and Stepan 1996a,b; Przeworski 1991). Though electoral integrity rests on a series of well-defined requirements (Birch 2011; van Ham 2014; Norris 2014, 2015; Norris et al. 2014; Schedler 2002), scholars generally agree that the concept of "fairness" is a crucial qualitative judgment that voters are in a position to make beyond these stricter definitions (Bowler et al. 2015; Mattes and Bratton 2007; Mauk 2020; McAllister and White 2011; Moehler 2009; Norris 2019). In this context, several researchers have examined the conditions under which the conduct of elections is likely to be perceived as fair and either engenders public confidence or, to the contrary, leads citizens to question the legitimacy of the electoral process (Birch 2008; Nadeau and Blais 1993; Norris 2017; Werner and Marien 2022). For example, the recent 2016 and 2020 presidential elections in the United States have highlighted that citizens' perceptions of the fairness of the electoral process are very important, even in well-established democracies (Norris et al. 2020).

There are, however, considerably fewer studies that have examined the interplay between citizens' perceptions of electoral fairness, macro-level indicators of electoral integrity, and satisfaction with democracy (Alemika 2007; Dahlberg and Linde 2016; Mauk 2020; McAllister and White 2011). Furthermore, few studies have analyzed the relationship between incidents of electoral fraud and contestation and citizens' satisfaction with the functioning of their democratic institutions across time and space (Fortin-Rittberger et al. 2017; Norris 2019). Finally, no systematic studies have been conducted on the relationship between the presence of electoral observers to ensure the integrity of the electoral process and SWD – but see Chernykh and Slovik (2015), Gafuri (2021), and Hyde and Marinov (2012, 2014) on the importance of electoral monitoring.

The understudied issues described here are addressed in this section, which is divided into three sections. First, we examine the distribution and key determinants of citizens' perceptions of the fairness of the electoral process. There are only few surveys that have directly measured these perceptions in a comparative perspective with an interesting amount of variance at the country level (e.g., Norris 2019). The second part of the section seeks to re-examine perceptions of the fairness of the electoral process through the prism of one of the most robust relationships observed in political science literature, that is, the winner–loser gap in SWD observed after elections (Anderson et al. 2005; Dahlberg and Linde 2016; Martini and Quaranta 2019; Nadeau and Blais 1993).

The third part of this section is devoted to the almost unexplored relationship between electoral monitoring and SWD. Examining this relationship is fundamental, as it directly addresses what has been defined as the "information problem" in emergent democracies. This issue refers to the lack of accurate information about the quality of the electoral process, making it difficult for citizens to evaluate which elections are fair and acceptable (Cantu and Garcia Ponce 2015; Carreras and Irepoglu 2013; Chernykh and Slovik 2015; Fearon 2011; Hyde and Marinov 2012, 2014). In this regard, electoral monitoring could play a key role by providing citizens with impartial information about the electoral process (from a third-party organization), which, in turn, will create incentives for governments to hold clean elections (Gafuri 2021; König et al. 2022; Norris et al. 2014; Norris 2019). Besides exerting a surveillance function on the conduct of elections, the presence of international observers to monitor national elections in emergent democracies thereby has the potential to affect citizens' views about the fairness of the electoral process and their level of satisfaction with their political regime.

The absence of studies measuring the effect of electoral fraud and monitoring on SWD is likely due to the lack of data. Hyde and Marinov's (2012, 2014, 2019) recent compilation of such a database now makes it possible to carry out such a study (see also Chernykh and Slovik 2015). The data produced by the National Elections Across Democracy and Autocracy Dataset project (Hyde and Marinov 2019) allow us to conduct the first systematic study on the relationship between electoral monitoring and SWD, which covers a long period of time and a large set of countries. The analysis in the third section of this section will therefore allow us, among other things, to determine if the effect of electoral monitoring on SWD varies across contexts.

To conduct these analyses, we use CSES data from module 1 when examining evaluations of the electoral process, and all five modules when analyzing satisfaction with democracy. For further details on the dataset, see Section 1. The results of this section will allow us to better understand the conditions under which perceptions about the fairness of the electoral process are most likely to affect citizens' SWD. These findings also have the potential to inform implications and recommendations on the effectiveness of the actions of national and international actors by positively affecting citizens' perceptions of the fairness of the electoral process and their level of satisfaction with the functioning of their democratic institutions.

2.2 Level and Determinants of Citizens' Perceptions about Electoral Fairness

For both political theorists and citizens, free and competitive elections, as well as transparency in the counting of votes cast are pillars of democracy and the electoral process. It then seems natural in this context that citizens' perceptions of the fairness of the electoral process appear as a critical component of citizens' overall satisfaction with the functioning of their democratic institutions (Birch 2008, 2011; Hyde and Marinov 2014; König et al. 2022; McAllister and White 2011; Mochtak et al. 2021; Norris 2013; Norris et al. 2014; Schedler 2002). It is therefore also not surprising that citizens, who are exposed to electoral violence (conceived as violent actions to influence the process and the outcome of an election), are less likely to exhibit strong support for democracy (Daxecker and Fjelde 2022).

Despite their centrality for SWD, citizens' perceptions of the fairness of the electoral process have rarely been measured using a comparable indicator that would allow for a series of cross-national, large-N, comparative analyses. In this section, we make use of a question in module 1 of the CSES surveys that asks respondents' opinions about the fairness of the last election held in their country. The precise wording of this question is as follows:

> In some countries, people believe their elections are conducted fairly. In other countries, people believe that their elections are conducted unfairly. Thinking of the last election in [country], where would you place yourself on this scale of one to five where ONE means that the last election was conducted fairly and FIVE means that the last election was conducted unfairly?

The distribution of the variable is shown in Figure 6. The overrepresentation of established democracies in the CSES (see Section 1 for a discussion on this point) surveys explains the skewed distribution toward positive evaluations. Indeed, more than 50 percent of respondents gave the highest score on the scale

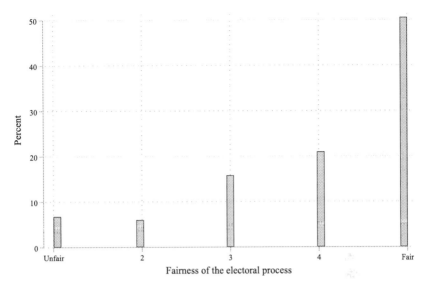

Figure 6 Distribution of the perceptions of the electoral process (fair election)
Note: $N = 51,619$.

for electoral fairness in their country's last election. That said, it is still interesting to note that nearly 30 percent of survey respondents gave relatively low scores of 3, 2, or 1 on the fairness scale, thereby providing an interesting deal of variance.

Our first goal in this section is to identify the main determinants of citizens' perceptions of electoral fairness. Previous work in this area suggests that these perceptions are well grounded in reality insofar as they should reflect citizens' ability to detect various manifestations of electoral fraud or malfeasance (Birch 2008, 2011; Fortin-Rittberger et al. 2017; McAllister and White 2011; Mochtak et al. 2021; Moehler 2009; Norris et al. 2014; Norris 2017, 2019; Werner and Marien 2022). These studies have also shown that winners tend to be overwhelmingly satisfied with the process through which the party or candidate they voted for was elected (Anderson et al. 2005; Nadeau et al. 2021). Based on the literature, two results should stand out. First, we should observe a systematic relationship between the objective quality of democratic institutions in a given country and citizens' perceptions of the fairness of the electoral process in the last election held. Second, we should also expect a strong positive link between having voted for the winning camp and holding a positive view of the electoral process that has produced this outcome.

The dependent variable in our first set of analysis is electoral fairness. The first key independent variable in our analysis is V-Dem's electoral democracy index (see Section 1 for details). Another important independent variable is the electoral status measure. We follow the conventional wisdom by conceiving winners as being voters who supported a party that ended up in the government. As put by Anderson et al. (2005: 33–34), "Theoretically speaking, winning and losing really are about a person's sense of allegiance to those in or out of power" and allows to "identify citizens' status as part of the electoral majority or minority." (Anderson et al. 2005: 33–34). For a review of the studies defending this view, see Daoust et al. (2023: 162–163). In particular, we should mention that Stiers et al.'s (2018) study, which includes questions that tap into what winning or losing an election means according to citizens themselves, supports this methodological choice. Hence, in line with the conventional wisdom, the authors showed that citizens conceive their electoral status (winner or loser) first and foremost in majoritarian terms (i.e., in or out of the government).[9] Thus, winners are coded 1 while losers and abstainers are coded 0.

Finally, our models include several individual control variables (age, gender, education, and income quintile), as well as macro-level variables measuring the level of economic inequality in a country (measured with the Gini index), its degree of wealth (measured by GDP per capita, adjusted based on purchasing power parity) and the electoral systems. We include these variables because we believe that they could reasonably act as confounders throughout our analysis (e.g., Aarts and Thomassen 2008; Anderson et al. 2005; Krieckhaus et al. 2014; Quaranta and Martini 2016).[10] A detailed description of the coding of the variables and their descriptive statistics are presented in Online Appendix C. Since the data have a nested structure, we estimate mixed-effect models with a two-level structure where individuals nested in elections nested in countries (Gelman and Hill 2006). We specify random intercepts at the election levels.

A first set of key results presented in Table 2 focus on the contextual factors that may influence citizens' perceptions of the integrity of the electoral process. Two results stand out. The first result concerns the existence of a positive, significant, and substantial link between the quality of electoral institutions in a country and the willingness of its citizens to believe that the last election was conducted in a fair manner. The second result, related to the first, is the absence of significant links between the evaluation of the electoral process and the economic conditions that prevail in a country, as measured by its level of economic development and economic inequality. These findings are important

---

[9] Of course, other factors can play, such as the relative performance compared to the previous election (e.g., Plescia 2019), the electoral outcome at the district level (instead of solely the national/government outcome) in countries with single-member districts (Daoust and Blais 2017; Ridge 2022: or the level of the election (Daoust et al. 2023)). But these factors matter less and matter for much fewer people.

[10] Removing the macro-level control variables from our models does not alter our conclusions.

Table 2 Mixed-effects linear model predicting citizens' perceptions of the electoral process

	Model 1
Age (years)	0.001***
	(0.000)
Sex (female = 1)	−0.023***
	(0.003)
Education	0.009***
	(0.001)
Income quintiles	0.040***
	(0.004)
Winner	0.066***
	(0.003)
Electoral democracy index	0.264**
	(0.099)
Gini	−0.002
	(0.003)
GDP per capita (PPP)	0.000
	(0.000)
Majoritarian (ref = mixed)	0.091*
	(0.044)
Proportional (ref = mixed)	0.101*
	(0.043)
Constant	0.402**
	(0.134)
σ^2 elections, intercept	−2.426***
	(0.127)
σ^2 residuals	−1.328***
	(0.004)
N (elections)	32
N (respondents)	38,809

Note: Standard errors in parentheses $^{*}p < 0.05$, $^{**}p < 0.01$, $^{***}p < 0.001$

as they clearly indicate that citizens' assessments of their electoral systems are grounded in reality, given the relationship with the V-Dem's measure of the quality of a political regime. Indeed, a large body of work has shown a very significant link between a country's level of development, as measured by the value of gross national product per capita, and citizens' SWD (Christmann 2018; Daoust and Nadeau 2021; Lühiste 2014; Nadeau et al. 2019). However, we do not see such a relationship in Table 2 when it comes to predicting citizens' perceptions of the electoral process (these results contrast the findings presented in the next section where the predicted outcome is SWD).

The individual determinant exerting the most influence on citizens' perceptions is, as expected, respondents' winning or losing status. This result suggests that the outcome of the election is a significant determinant of voters' judgments about the fairness of the electoral system, which in turn, as we shall see in the next section, is a central dimension of citizens' overall satisfaction with the functioning of their democratic institutions. This initial set of findings is both important and worrisome since it implies that many citizens assess the quality of the electoral process through the outcome it produces rather than through its integrity and fairness.

The results presented so far are insightful in that they help shape our understanding of the factors explaining citizens' perceptions of the fairness of the electoral system, a central pillar of democratic institutions. Two key results emerge from this perspective, one related to the individual winner or loser status of respondents, and the other, which refers to a contextual factor, that is, the objective quality of electoral institutions in a given country. The possible interplay between these two factors could suggest that the winner–loser gap in the appreciation of the electoral process could vary according to the quality of democracy between countries. We examine this in the subsequent section.

2.3 Electoral Outcomes and Perceptions of Electoral Fairness across Quality of Democracy

Several strands of research suggest that winners' and losers' assessments of the fairness of the electoral process differ in low- and high-quality democracies. This difference is also reflected in work exploring the effect of citizens' assessments of the fairness of the electoral process on their level of satisfaction with democracy. For instance, Moehler (2009: 360) concludes that "winner status in Africa is positively related to the perception of a free and fair election [and] has the largest influence on evaluations of electoral integrity in both substantive and statistical terms." Moreover, Carreras and Irepoglu (2013: 610) note that "trust in elections is quite low in Latin America" and conclude that the presence of irregularities that characterized the electoral processes in this region may explain losers' inclination "[to denounce] that the elections had been manipulated by the incumbent government" (Carreras and Irepoglu 2013). McAllister and White (2011) reach a similar conclusion about elections in Russia.

The foregoing observations suggesting that we should expect a substantial gap in the fairness assessment of the electoral process between winners and losers in established and emerging democracies rest on solid theoretical foundations. First, this expectation is consistent with numerous studies showing that voters operate as motivated reasoners by paying attention to congruent information or by explaining away incongruent messages (Kernell and Mullinix 2019; Kunda 1990; Lodge and Taber 2000). This expectation is also in line with the widely recognized notion that oriented information quests do not take place in a vacuum (Kernell and Mullinix 2019; Lodge and Taber 2013). Hence, across time and space, motivated reasoners are likely exposed to different dosages of evidence that either comfort or challenge their existing beliefs and evaluations about the election outcome. We argue that the observed variation in the size of the winner–loser gap in assessments of the fairness of electoral outcomes crucially depends on the interaction between an individual psychological process, motivated reasoning, and the differences in the information environment in low- and high-quality democracies (Nadeau et al. 2021).

The notion that information environment varies with the quality of democracy is neatly supported in the literature. First, many researchers have suggested that a democracy is "self-reinforcing" when competing parties, and most evidently losers, prefer the outcome of elections over the violence that could otherwise ensue if they refuse to accept a defeat.[11] Second, incentives for parties to engage in electoral fraud or to raise doubts about the fairness of the electoral process differ markedly in high- and low-quality democracies. Hyde and Marinov (2014) show that fraudulent elections and overt defiance of electoral results are rarely witnessed in established democracies because the probability of being caught is large, while the consequences of being portrayed as sore losers may be highly detrimental. In brief, because parties have no interest in stealing or contesting elections in high-quality democracies, contestations are rare and the media typically has limited to report about these types of events – while the opposite is true in low-quality democracies.

The preceding arguments suggest that the quality of democracy should affect both the amount and the diversity of available information related to electoral fairness (Daxecker et al. 2019; Moehler 2009; Norris 2017, 2019; Norris et al. 2014). In low-quality democracies, losers will be exposed to larger amounts and more diverse pieces of information that could strengthen their doubts about the fairness of the electoral system. The opposite is likely to be true in high-quality democracies. In the absence of information that questions the integrity of the election, partisans of defeated candidates are more likely to accept the outcome of the election and "lose happily" (Dahlberg and Linde 2016). For winners, we

---

[11] On the notion of self-reinforcing democracy, see Prezworski (2005, 2008) and Apolte (2018). Specifically concerning elections as "self-enforcing mechanisms," see Fearon (2011), Hyde and Marinov (2014), and Chernykh and Slovik (2015).

expect a similar effect of motivated reasoning, which amplifies effects of the election outcomes across contexts. Contrary to emerging democracies, winners in established democracies are less likely to be exposed to information and cues that will prompt them to interpret the victory as the most decisive indication of the fairness of the electoral process.

The considerations above predict a substantial gap in the assessment of the electoral process between winners and losers in established and emerging democracies. This expectation has never been systematically tested using a direct measure of perceptions of the fairness of the electoral system obtained across a diverse set of countries that vary in their development and the maturity of their democratic institutions. The CSES module 1 data allow us to execute such a test, requiring the addition of an interaction term to the model presented in Table 2.

The results of the relationship between the quality of democracy and the size of the winner–loser gap are presented in Table 3. First, we note the presence of a significant gap between winners and losers in less established democracies, as attested by the coefficients on the winner variable. This result therefore confirms the close link between winner–loser status and perceptions about the integrity of the electoral process in emerging democracies. The magnitude of this gap highlights the important challenges of building widespread trust in the fairness of the electoral system in emerging democracies, particularly among voters on the losing side.

The most important result in Table 3 concerns the estimate of the interaction between the quality of democracy and the winner–loser status on evaluations of the fairness of the electoral process. To illustrate the effects, we plot the average marginal effect of winning in Figure 7. The magnitude of the winner–loser gap on the integrity of the electoral system varies substantially with the quality of democracy in a given country. The results show that this gap, which reaches almost 0.31 on a scale of 0 to 1 in emerging democracies, is very close (0.02) to zero in well-established democracies. This indicates that trust in the electoral system is largely confined to winners in low-quality democracies, whereas, in high-quality democracies, it exists among both winners and losers.

The results in Table 3 and Figure 7 imply that the proportion and distribution between winners and losers satisfied with the electoral system varies markedly with the quality of democracy. This conditional effect is revealing in itself. For instance, it could explain why SWD is higher in established democracies since perceptions of the fairness of the electoral process systematically and substantially affect citizens' SWD.[12] The results in Table 3, which present the findings

---

[12] The most comprehensive study to date was conducted by Pipa Norris who used data from the World Values Survey. Using several indicators measuring citizens' perceptions about the conduct of elections in forty-two countries between 2010 and 2014, Norris (2019: 5) concludes

Table 3 The interaction of winning and quality of democracy on electoral fairness

	Model 1
Electoral democracy index × Winner	-0.408^{***}
	(0.017)
Winner	0.416^{***}
	(0.090)
Electoral democracy index	0.456^{***}
	(0.110)
Age (years)	0.001^{***}
	(0.000)
Sex (female=1)	-0.025^{***}
	(0.003)
Education	0.010^{***}
	(0.001)
Income quintiles	0.042^{***}
	(0.004)
Gini	-0.000
	(0.003)
GDP per capita (PPP)	0.000
	(0.000)
Majoritarian	0.058
	(0.049)
Proportional	0.087
	(0.048)
Constant	0.204
	(0.150)
σ^2 elections, winner	-2.256^{***}
	(0.135)
σ^2 elections, intercept	-2.317^{***}
	(0.127)
σ^2 residuals	-1.349^{***}
	(0.004)
N (elections)	32
N (respondents)	38,809

Note: Mixed-effects linear model predicting citizens' perceptions of the electoral process. Standard errors in parentheses $^{*}p < 0.05$, $^{**}p < 0.01$, $^{***}p < 0.001$

"doubts about electoral integrity do indeed undermine general satisfaction with how democracy works.". Our results concur with Norris' findings based on different indicators, time period, and sample of countries.

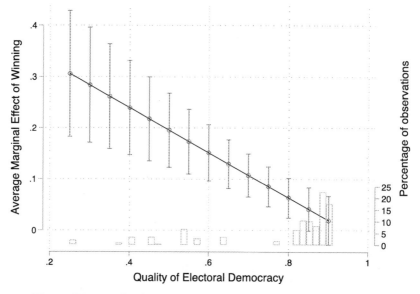

Figure 7 Interaction between winner/loser and quality of democracy

of a mixed-effects linear model predicting SWD,[13] confirm this presumption. The explanatory variables are the same as those used in the model measuring perceptions about the electoral system, which are also included in the analysis. The key finding in this table concerns the strong relationship between the satisfaction with the functioning of the electoral system and democratic institutions in general. As Figure 8 shows, the level of SWD is boosted by almost 0.25 (on a 0 to 1 scale) for citizens who firmly believe that the last election in their country was conducted fairly. This expected result supports the idea that the relatively low proportion of citizens believing in the fairness of the electoral process within low-quality democracies could explain why the level of satisfaction with democracy is significantly lower in this context compared to established democracies.

Moreover, the distribution of citizens' satisfaction according to their winner–loser status provides insight into the workings of the same type of winner–loser gap that has been consistently observed in the literature regarding the determinants of SWD. The data presented in Figure 9 are revealing in this respect. First, when comparing democracies above the median score on quality of democracy (i.e., 0.854), with those below, Figure 9 shows that the gap between the evaluations of the electoral process between winners and losers varies significantly between emergent and established democracies. These differences are notably explained

---

[13] For a description of this variable, see Section 1.

Table 4 Electoral fairness and satisfaction with democracy

	Model 1
Age (years)	−0.000
	(0.000)
Sex (female=1)	−0.005[*]
	(0.003)
Education	0.001
	(0.001)
Income quintiles	0.041[***]
	(0.004)
Winner	0.037[***]
	(0.003)
Electoral democracy index	0.108
	(0.064)
Electoral fairness	0.234[***]
	(0.005)
Gini	0.003
	(0.002)
GDP per capita (PPP)	0.000[***]
	(0.000)
Majoritarian	0.081[**]
	(0.028)
Proportional	0.054[*]
	(0.027)
Constant	−0.022
	(0.086)
σ^2 elections, intercept	−2.877[***]
	(0.129)
σ^2 residuals	−1.414[***]
	(0.004)
N (elections)	32
N (respondents)	37463

Note: Standard errors in parentheses [*] $p < 0.05$, [**] $p < 0.01$, [***] $p < 0.001$

by the significantly higher proportion of losers, who are unsatisfied with the electoral process, compared to those who are dissatisfied in high- and low-quality democracies. That is, 43 percent of losers express rather negative views (scores of 1, 2, or 3) about the fairness of the electoral process in democracies of lower quality, compared to only 20 percent in democracies of higher quality (top panel of Figure 9). These figures suggest that the significant differences between winners

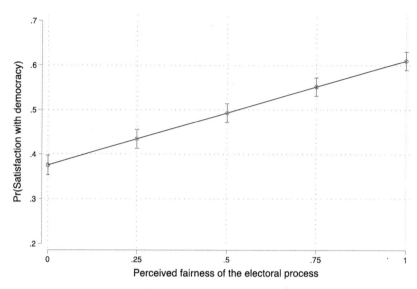

Figure 8 Satisfaction with democracy and perceived fairness of electoral
process

Note: 95 percent confidence intervals included. Estimations based on Table 4.

and losers regarding the fairness of the electoral system in low- and high-quality
democracies, which are large in the former case and much less pronounced in the
latter, could go a long way towards explaining the emergence of a winner–loser
gap in the level of SWD in emerging and established democracies.

The results presented in this section provide revealing insights. First, the
findings established that the determinants of satisfaction with the electoral
process were more circumscribed and narrowly political than those that would
influence citizens' broader satisfaction with democratic institutions as a whole.
They then showed that the electoral status and the objective quality of democratic processes in a given country were the key factors explaining citizens'
perceptions of the integrity of the electoral process. This indicates that these
perceptions are grounded in reality, which provides us with a first clue in
explaining the differences in SWD in established and emerging democracies.
The most striking results in this section, however, concern the impact of the
interaction between the winner–loser status and the quality of democracy on
individuals' perceptions of the fairness of the electoral process. These results
revealed a significantly larger winner–loser gap with regard to perceived electoral process fairness in emerging compared to established democracies. This
finding is important on several levels. First, it provides a better understanding of
the more global phenomenon of the winner–loser gap in SWD. Second, it
reveals the magnitude of the challenge of consolidating confidence in the

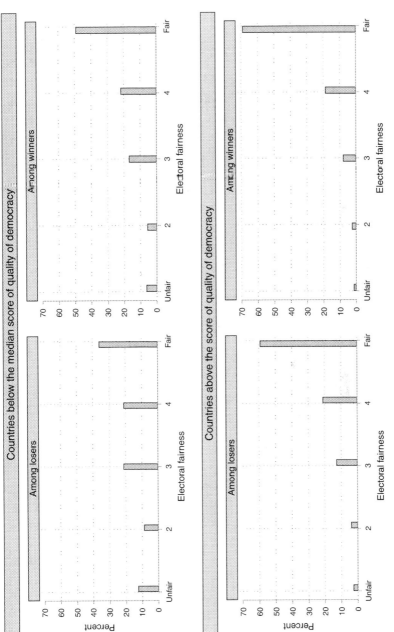

Figure 9 Winning, losing, and satisfaction with the electoral process in low-quality democracies

electoral process in emerging democracies. In the next section, we turn specifically to the study of a mechanism put in place to achieve this objective: electoral monitoring.

2.4 Electoral Monitoring and Satisfaction with Democracy

The results of the previous section, as well as the important work of Norris (2019), show a strong, systematic, and substantial link between citizens' perceptions of the integrity of the electoral process and their satisfaction with the functioning of democracy. However, to our knowledge, no study has systematically examined the possible link between election monitoring and SWD. This section fills this somewhat surprising gap. To the extent that the presence of international observers is intended to strengthen citizens' confidence in the integrity of the electoral process, and given the demonstrated link between perceptions of fairness and SWD (Norris 2019), it is plausible to hypothesize that election monitoring should have a positive and significant impact on individuals' evaluations of the functioning of their democratic system.[14]

The arguments and findings from the previous section suggest that factors that are likely to reassure citizens about the fairness of the electoral process should also have a positive effect on their level of SWD. Numerous studies have shown that attempts at electoral fraud are both costly and risky (Beaulieu and Hyde 2009; Saikkonen and White 2021; Schedler 2002; Simpser 2013; Skovoroda and Lankina 2017). These studies have convincingly shown that the presence of foreign observers is an effective constraint limiting electoral manipulation, by raising the costs and risks associated with such practices, a conclusion aptly summarized by Saikkonen and White (2021: 161), who note that "autocratic regimes target electoral manipulation where they have the greatest capacity to do so." It therefore seems reasonable to expect that the presence of election observers sends a strong signal to citizens that attempts at manipulation in a given election will be reduced and that the electoral process will be fairer, which should have a positive effect on their level of SWD.

There are also good reasons to believe that the presence of electoral observers will matter more in low-quality democracies. First, one may argue that the "information problem" previously discussed is likely to be more acute in emerging democracies because of the polarization of losers and winners on this issue and the absence in many cases of impartial and autonomous institutions supervising the proper conduct of elections (Cantu and Garcia Ponce 2015; Carreras and Irepoglu 2013; Chernykh and Slovik 2015; Fearon 2011; Hyde and Marinov 2012, 2014).

---

[14] This line of reasoning assumes, however, that organizations monitoring the elections reach the same conclusion regarding the electoral process, which is usually (although not always) the case (Daxecker and Schneider 2014).

Furthermore, low-quality democracies are characterized by an incumbent's informational advantage due to the government's control over the vote count and the release of results, which is susceptible to produce, according to Chernykh and Slovik (2015: 408): "a failure of self-enforcing democracy." Second, there are good reasons to believe that the issue of electoral integrity will be more salient in low-quality democracies. This expectation seems highly plausible given the well-recognized role of contextual factors in citizens' information environment. For instance, Rohrschneider and Loveless (2010: 1034) showed that "macro conditions affect the [national] information environment." Though this macro perspective has been mostly used to predict under which conditions citizens rely on economic or political considerations when assessing their level of satisfaction with democracy (Daoust and Nadeau 2021; Rohrschneider and Loveless 2010), the argument is of general scope. Indeed, Dahlberg et al. (2015: 27) also make this case when they claim that "different types of democracies face different challenges and we may assume that this has consequences for explanations of democratic discontent." Based on these insights, we argue that the presence of electoral observers will carry more weight on citizens' perceptions about the quality of elections and the adequate functioning of their political institutions in emergent democracies than is the case in established ones.

    The lack of studies on the impact of electoral monitoring on SWD can be explained, as mentioned earlier, by the lack of comprehensive datasets. The dataset compiled on this topic by Hyde and Marinov (2012, 2014, 2019) from 1945 to 2021 offers the possibility of including this information for 180 elections that took place between 1996 and 2020, all of which are included in the CSES.[15] The variable from the NELDA dataset (version 6.0) that will be leveraged in this section is the outcome of a literature review that answers the question, "Were international observers present?" The NELDA data show that election observers were deployed in just over one-third (35 percent) of the elections included in the CSES. The data also indicate that the deployment of international observers was greater in emerging democracies, as well as in the context of elections where concerns about their impartiality had been expressed.[16]

---

[15] The data used in this section originate from the Codebook for National Elections Across Democracy Dataset, 6.0, compiled by Susan Hyde and Nikolay Marinov, which was made available on July 23, 2021. For a full description of the methodology used to capture the context in which these elections were conducted, see Hyde and Marinov (2012) as well as the codebook version of the NELDA project presented above – see their publicly available website.

[16] The correlation between the presence of international observers (NELDA45) and V-Dem's indicator of polyarchy index is −0.36 (Pearson's r). The correlation between the deployment of international observers and the presence of concerns about the integrity of the electoral process (NELDA11: "Before elections, are there significant concerns that elections will not be free and fair?") is 0.33. These relatively moderate correlations are reassuring because they do not seem to indicate a severe collinearity problem, which could lead to a significant bias in the

An analysis of the effect of election monitoring on SWD is presented in Table 5. The following two estimates are added to the model: electoral monitoring, which takes the value of 1 when international observers are deployed during an election and 0 otherwise, and an interactive variable between electoral monitoring and quality of democracy.

The results confirm these expectations and show that the relationship between election monitoring and SWD varies greatly according to the quality of a democratic system. This pattern is illustrated by Figure 10, which suggests

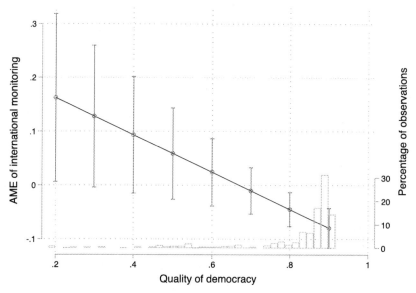

Figure 10 Interaction international monitoring and quality of electoral democracy

Note: 95 percent confidence intervals included. Estimations based on Table 5

---

estimation of the effect of electoral monitoring on SWD (Greene 2012). Another potential problem in estimating this effect is endogeneity. We argue that there are good theoretical reasons to believe that it is the observation of electoral irregularities at time t that is likely to lead to the presence of more extensive election monitoring at time $t+1$ for a variety of reasons (Beaulieu and Hyde 2009; Lehoucq 2003; Schedler 2013; Saikkonen and White 2021). This increased presence of electoral observers would likely lead voters to conclude that the electoral process is more equitable, leading them to express greater satisfaction with the functioning of democracy in their country. Election monitoring would thus play a dual role. The presence of foreign observers would signal citizens that their government both recognizes that the electoral process needs to be improved and that it has taken the necessary steps to do so. Of course, more refined measures of election monitoring would allow for a more refined measurement of the effect of election monitoring on citizens' perceptions (see Saikkonen and White 2021). The results presented in this section should be thought of as a first step in the study of the complex links between electoral monitoring and citizens' SWD.

Table 5 Electoral monitoring and satisfaction with democracy

	Model 1
Electoral democracy index × International monitors	-0.346^{**}
	(0.126)
International monitors	0.232^{*}
	(0.104)
Electoral democracy index	0.279^{*}
	(0.122)
Age (years)	0.000^{***}
	(0.000)
Sex (female=1)	-0.008^{***}
	(0.001)
Education	0.006^{***}
	(0.001)
Income quintiles	0.052^{***}
	(0.002)
Winner	0.070^{***}
	(0.001)
Gini	0.001
	(0.001)
GDP per capita (PPP)	0.000^{***}
	(0.000)
Majoritarian	0.049^{*}
	(0.021)
Proportional	0.001
	(0.018)
Constant	0.033
	(0.114)
σ^2 elections, monitor	-2.919^{***}
	(0.363)
σ^2 elections, intercept	-2.427^{***}
	(0.071)
σ^2 residuals	-1.336^{***}
	(0.002)
N (elections)	188
N (respondents)	209,768

Note: Standard errors in parentheses $^{*}p < 0.05$, $^{**}p < 0.01$, $^{***}p < 0.001$

that electoral monitoring has a positive effect on citizens' satisfaction with their democratic institutions precisely when the deployment of international observers is most likely to solve the problem of information access in the integrity of the electoral process, i.e., in emerging democracies. The effects observed may appear to be quite limited, given the scale of the resources devoted to election monitoring. However, it should be kept in mind that the effects observed in this case most likely underestimate the positive effect of electoral monitoring, which is also exerted through its impact on perceptions of the integrity of the electoral process, an important determinant of SWD. Overall, this section's analysis of the effect of election monitoring on satisfaction with democracy suggests that the deployment of international observers in emerging democracies produces the expected results.[17]

2.5 Conclusion

For many citizens, free and fair elections represent the foundations of democracy. It therefore seemed logical to begin our investigation with the relationship between elections and individuals' satisfaction with the functioning of their democratic institutions, by examining their perceptions of the fairness of the electoral process in their country. This study was conducted primarily using data from module 1 of the CSES, the only module explicitly measuring these perceptions.

The results presented in this section appear both important and insightful. We were able to establish that perceptions about electoral process integrity are strongly rooted in reality, as evidenced by the strong link between these perceptions and the "objective" quality of democratic institutions in a country. Importantly, not only were we able to demonstrate that voters who supported the winning side were more satisfied with the way the elections in their country were conducted, but that this relationship was also strongly conditioned by the quality of democratic institutions. The uncovering of this winner–loser gap in perceptions of electoral fairness, and especially the demonstration that the size of this gap varied considerably according to the quality of the democracy, is important for two reasons.

First, these results shed light on one of the most robust relationships uncovered in the study of political attitudes, namely the emergence of a winner–loser gap in satisfaction with the functioning of democracy (Anderson and Guillory 1997; Anderson et al. 2005; Blais and Gélineau 2007; Curini et al. 2012; Nadeau and Blais 1993; Nadeau et al. 2019, 2021). Second, the close link between winner–loser status and perceptions about the integrity of the electoral

---

[17] It would have been preferable to study the entire chain of effects, taking into account the direct and indirect effects (through perceptions of the fairness of the electoral process) of electoral monitoring on satisfaction with democracy, but data limitations prevent us from doing so.

process, a pillar of satisfaction with democracy, shows the extent to which "the information problem" about the fair and equitable conduct of elections is particularly severe in emerging democracies. Insofar as the deployment of election observers is often presented as an important part of the solution to this problem (Chernykh and Slovik 2015; Gafuri 2021; Garnett 2019; Hyde and Marinov 2012; 2014; Mauk 2020; Norris 2019), it seemed important to try to establish for the first time the existence of a link between election monitoring and SWD. The results presented in this section have shown the existence of such an effect in the most desirable context, that is, of emerging democracies.

The results presented in this section open up a series of avenues that we will now continue to explore in greater depth in the following two sections. These analyses will allow us to gain greater understanding of the nature of the links between the conduct of elections, the results they produce, and citizens' satisfaction with the functioning of their democratic system.

3 Processes, Outcomes, and Quality of Democracy

3.1 Introduction

Elections affect citizens' level of political support in numerous ways. For instance, as covered in the previous section, perceptions of the electoral process (i.e., fairness) are crucial. Moreover, the experience of democracy in practice, such as going to vote at a polling station (Kostelka and Blais 2018), and the outputs generated from elections, are known to influence satisfaction with democracy (Anderson et al. 2005). Furthermore, elections provide an opportunity for citizens to hold politicians accountable, which is essential in a liberal democracy. This accountability provides incentives for elected representatives to be responsive to citizens' preferences and demands, and the extent to which citizens believe that their government is responsive, in turn, shapes their SWD (Linz and Stepan 1996a, 1996b; Huang et al. 2008). Overall, elections are expected to be free and fair, to materialize citizens' votes into representation, and to serve as a mechanism to keep governments responsive to citizens' demands (Dahl 1998; Linz and Stepan 1996a, 1996b; Powell 2004; Przeworski 1991).

Although all these factors are important in shaping citizens' evaluations of their country's political system, they are very different in nature. Nonetheless, we can distinguish between two general types of considerations: *process-* and *output*-oriented factors. On the one hand, process-oriented considerations relate to features, such as the extent to which the campaign was fair, citizens' perceptions that electoral participation matters for democracy, and that campaigning parties care about what citizens think. On the other hand, some considerations are strictly output-oriented. They are independent of the electoral process and, instead, rely on electoral results. Examples include which party wins key positions (president, lower or upper house majority, etc.), the size of the victory and the loss, as well as other similar factors. Whether a voter ends up on the winning or the losing side (i.e., in or out of the government) is, however, the key output-related consideration (Anderson et al. 2005; Stiers et al. 2018).

A limited but insightful strand of research suggests that citizens' evaluation of electoral institutions is more process-oriented in established democracies and more output-related in emergent democracies (Dahlberg et al. 2015; Kittilson and Anderson 2011; Lührmann et al. 2017; Reher 2015). This observation does not mean, as demonstrated in Section 1, that the factors guiding citizens' assessments of how democracy works in practice are fundamentally different in different countries. What this contextual effect might reveal instead is that the "macro" conditions that prevail in low- and high-quality democracies could impact the relative weight of the various types of political considerations entering citizens' judgments about the performance of their democratic institutions (Christmann 2018; Nadeau et al. 2023; Rohrschneider and Loveless 2010). According to Dahlberg et al. (2015: 31) for instance, "the factors that make democrats dissatisfied are to a large extent conditioned by the level of institutional consolidation," an observation which leads them to note that "subjective assessments of being represented matter more in democracies with well-functioning institutions" (2015: 27). Reher (2015: 163) argues similarly that when the basic requirements of democracy such as free and fair elections are not fulfilled "they should be more salient in citizens' evaluations of the functioning of their democratic system . . . In contrast, if the fundamental elements of democracy are in place, citizens are likely to focus on processes such as elite's representation of, and responsiveness to, citizens' concerns."

Despite these well-founded observations, we still know relatively little about the conditions under which one type of consideration will prevail over another in citizens' judgments about the performance of their democratic system. In this section, we seek to provide such an analysis by showing that the extent to which the requisites of liberal democracy are achieved in a given country is the key factor shaping the relative weight of process- or output-related political considerations in citizens' assessments of democracies.

To do so, we leverage data from the Comparative Study of Electoral Systems, which cover all five modules (more than 200 elections across fifty-seven different countries from 1996 to 2020). Our results show that, overall, citizens in democracies of higher quality rely to a greater extent on process-oriented considerations (compared to citizens in democracies of lower quality). On the contrary, the quality of a democratic regime moderates the impact of output-related factors in such a way that these factors matter more in countries where democratic institutions are of lower quality. At the end of this section, we discuss the methodological implications of our findings for large-N comparative analyses of SWD, as well as the normative implications related to the nature of citizens' assessment of their political institutions.

The results presented in this section make several contributions. First, the findings add to our understanding of the link between electoral status (winner or loser) and SWD (e.g., Anderson and Guillory 1997; Dahlberg et al. 2015) by uncovering the context under which the winner–loser gap prevails over other political considerations. Such an analysis is only possible thanks to the great deal of variation in the quality of democratic institutions provided by the CSES. Second, it reinforces the notion that determinants of SWD have heterogeneous effects across political contexts and emphasizes the need to put forward a methodological approach that seriously integrates context (Anderson et al. 2005; Dahlberg et al. 2015; Dahlberg and Linde, 2016; Reher 2015). Third, it connects arguments from various strands of literature to offer a better account of the circumstances determining the relative weight of political considerations in citizens' assessments of their political institutions. Lastly, it derives normative implications from these findings for the vitality of democracy and the nature of citizens' evaluations.

3.2 Process- and Output-Oriented Sources of Satisfaction with Democracy

Although many social scientists have focused on performance theories as conceived in economic terms, scholars have more recently shown that citizens' evaluations of their democratic institutions also depend on the production of a "diffuse basket of political goods," such as freedom and responsiveness (Huang et al. 2008: 51). The electoral process is intimately related to these considerations. Elections are expected to be free and fair, have inclusive suffrage, and serve as a mechanism to keep governments responsive to citizens' demands (Dahl 1989; Linz and Stepan 1996a, 1996b; Powell 2004; Przeworski 1991). Without elections, governments cannot be rewarded or punished and would thereby have little incentive to be responsive. Hence, it is not surprising that perceptions of electoral fairness are crucial in citizens' evaluations of their democratic regime, as shown in Section 2 (see also Magalhães 2016). A free and fair process allows citizens, particularly losers, to believe that they can win the next election if they come up with the best campaign and ideas (Nadeau and Blais 1993). They therefore have strong incentives to accept the (democratic) rules of the game.

Despite the centrality of the electoral process, citizens also attribute a lot of importance to what happens in-between elections. It is rather intuitive and reasonable to assume that citizens expect their government to not only implement the pledges they were elected for, but to also be responsive to public opinion. In fact, responsiveness to the electorate (that is, acting based on citizens' preferences) is a crucial factor for citizens when it comes to evaluating how elected representatives should act (Werner 2019). In fact, it is even more important than other key considerations, such as whether the representative pledged to enact a given policy during the campaign or the personal opinion of politicians (Dassonneville et al. 2021). In other words, citizens are more satisfied with democracy when politicians care about their preferences, and political parties take these into account when enacting public policies. This is in line with studies showing that citizens' beliefs about their elected officials' responsiveness play an important role in their evaluations of their democratic regime (Anderson et al. 2005; Norris 2014, 2019; Reher 2015). However, whether or not these considerations (that tap on to the notion of responsiveness and the process of the electoral systems) have a homogenous effect on political support is unclear. Hence, focusing on an average effect from a variety of contexts and generalizing it might be misleading.

Previous work showing that individuals assess their political institutions differently across contexts provides useful insights on this issue (Bratton and Mattes 2001; Miller et al. 1997). Important studies have demonstrated that citizens in emergent democracies seem to understand and evaluate democracy in more instrumental and less process-centered ways (Dalton et al. 2007; Norris, 2011). According to Reher (2015: 163): "fundamental elements of democracy include free and fair elections with inclusive suffrage and freedom of expression and association," a fundamental notion which leads her to conclude that "in places where these rights and institutions are not taken for granted, they should be most salient in citizens' evaluations of the functioning of their democratic system."

Building from these works, we hypothesize that citizens' shifting emphasis on different subsets of considerations in assessing their political institutions chiefly depends on a country's quality of democracy. This conjecture appears reasonable given that the electoral process in low-quality democracies is more likely to be framed as a "window dressing exercise for authoritarian politics" while it is usually praised in its high-quality counterparts as an efficient and fair mechanism "to ensure that political rulers are . . . accountable to the electorate" (Lührmann et al. 2017: 1). As a result, citizens in low-quality democracies are more exposed to the idea that electoral outcomes are unfair and invite scrutiny, whereas citizens in high-quality democracies are more so faced with the notion that election results are fair and should be gracefully accepted to preserve a valuable process efficient at solving power struggles peacefully and making governments responsive (Anderson and Mendes 2005; Bowler 2016; Moehler 2009). In brief, a country's quality of democracy appears to be a key contextual feature in determining the salience of various considerations entering citizens' judgments about the performance of their democratic institutions.

A large body of work provides insights into why citizens in emerging democracies will often attach greater importance to election results as a key indicator of whether or not democratic institutions are working well. In our previous section, we showed that many citizens in low-quality democracies carry doubts about the fairness of the electoral process, which are less widespread in established democracies (Birch 2008; Cantu and Garcia Ponce 2015; Carreras and Irepoglu 2013; Karp et al. 2018; Mauk 2020; Norris 2014, 2017, 2019; Norris et al. 2014; Werner and Marrien 2022). Skepticism about the conduct of elections in low quality democracies is often accompanied by concerns about the willingness of elected governments to be responsive to the needs of the population at large, including voters who cast ballots for losers. The endemic presence of corruption (Donovan and Karp 2017; Ferrin 2016; Wagner et al. 2009), clientelism practices (Dahlberg et al. 2015; Keefer 2007; Nadeau et al. 2017), and government control over the media (Stockman 2012; Gehlbach and Sonin 2014; Lührman 2017; Repucci 2019) are all factors that could bring losers in emerging democracies to conclude that incumbent governments will be mainly beholden to their supporters and special interest groups rather than to the population at large. The contrast is striking in established democracies. Indeed, losers seem to attach less importance to the results of elections, because they feel that the electoral process is fair, and, at the same time, are sensitive to the functioning of the mechanisms (media, parliaments, etc.) as ways of making their voices heard by governments after the elections have taken place (Nadeau et al. 2021).

The preceding observations have sought to make sense of the "expectation gap" between winners and losers, by predicting that it should be smaller in high-quality democracies. Furthermore, citizens in well-established democracies are reminded that newly elected governments are constantly scrutinized under checks and balances (through opposition groups in parliament, an independent press, guaranteed rights to express discontent through demonstrations, petitions, etc.), which prevents them from being exclusively responsive to their partisans. In brief, losers in well-established democracies have good reasons to think that they have lost fair and square and are invited, notably by the leader of their party,[18] to recall that they may be tomorrow's winners (Przeworski, 1991). Voters in high-quality democracies are thus incentivized to think of democracy

---

[18] The 2020 US presidential election was, of course, an exception that stands in sharp contrast to this expectation given that the country is considered as a high-quality democracy.

as a set of rules whose applications over an extended time horizon will make governments accountable and responsive to their demands (e.g., Dahl 1998).

Hence, the dominant criterion (among process- and output-related considerations) used by citizens to assess the performance of their democratic institutions should be context-specific. This is consistent with work showing that citizens tend to evaluate their political system based on its most salient aspects (Citrin et al. 2014; Rohrschneider and Loveless 2010). It also complements the "expectancy value" model, which characterizes political attitudes as a sum of considerations whose weights are largely determined by information environments (Chong and Druckman 2007). It is further consistent with the literature showing that citizens' perceptions about issues are grounded in reality (Anderson and Tverdova 2003; Dennison 2019; Nadeau et al. 2013).

Recent work sustains the notion that citizens' judgements of their political institutions are indeed more process-oriented in high-quality democracies. For instance, Dahlberg et al. (2015: 23) conclude that "in old democracies with well-functioning representative institutions and stable party systems, subjective assessments of being politically represented are more important than in new democracies." This insightful study is, however, limited to a single module of the CSES (i.e., module 2, 2001–6), and only to democratic countries (according to Freedom House). Moreover, the authors focus on "old" and "new" democracies (while we will focus on V-Dem's index tapping the quality of a democracy).

Overall, we argue that the relative weights of the political considerations influencing citizens' evaluation of their political regime are substantially determined by the quality of democracy. In high-quality democracies, individuals' levels of SWD should be (1) less affected by punctual electoral outcomes and (2) more driven by perceptions of electoral accountability, that is, politicians' responsiveness. The opposite patterns are expected to hold true in low-quality democracies. These two expectations can be summarized by the following hypotheses:

Hypothesis 1: The weight of process-related considerations (e.g., attitudes toward electoral responsiveness) on citizens' levels of SWD increases as the quality of a democracy increases.

Hypothesis 2: The weight of output-related considerations (e.g., being on the winning side) on citizens' levels of SWD decreases as the quality of a democracy increases.

Recent elections are neatly aligned with this theoretical framework. For example, the Canadian election of 2021, held in a well-established democracy, led to a one-party government formed by the Liberal party who lost the popular vote for the second time in a row. Despite this "reversed legitimacy" or "electoral inversion" (Carey et al. 2021), which opens the door to questions about the legitimacy of who should govern (we come back to this point in Section 4), no question or issue was raised about the main output-related factor: the Liberal party won most seats, and was thus entitled to form a government (and did so, remaining in power). Instead, the most important controversies about the elections were about the electoral process. More precisely, it focused on the fairness of the official leaders' debates and whether the moderators were biased in their questions (Blais and Daoust 2021). This is a clear case that aligns with our hypothesis that process-oriented considerations will trump output-oriented factors in citizens' evaluations of their political institutions in democracies of high quality. In the next section, we describe how we provide a systematic test of our hypotheses.

3.3 Data and Indicators

Like the other sections of this Element, we leverage datasets from the CSES datasets. For a discussion on the data please refer to Section 1. In the first set of tests for this section we use survey questions that were included in all five modules of the CSES. In the second set of tests, we focus on a more detailed analysis of process-oriented factors by making use of questions asked in module 1 only.

To capture a general sense of responsiveness as a key process-related consideration, we focus on what has been previously labeled as "political efficacy." The question reads as follows: "Some people say that no matter who people vote for, it won't make any difference to what happens. Others say that what people vote for can make a difference to what happens. Using the scale on this card (where one means that voting won't make a difference to what happens and 5 means that voting can make a difference), where would you place yourself?" The theoretical richness of this widely used survey question is well recognized. Among others, Aarts and Thomassen (2008: 9) refer to it as tapping "perceptions of accountability" whereas Kittilson and Anderson (2011: 35) interpret it as a measure of external efficacy which "measures citizens' sense that their participation matters to the political process and that elections lead to responsiveness to citizens demands."

To measure the most important output-related criterion, we focus on the winner–loser gap, which has been vastly studied and briefly examined in Section 2. The relationship between voting for a winning (or losing) party and having more positive (or negative) political attitudes, such as SWD, is one of the most robust relationships in political science. In this section, we follow the conventional wisdom, neatly tested and confirmed by Stiers et al. (2018), who show that winning is first and foremost about whether one votes for a governing party or not. Hence, we code a voter who supported a winning party that is part of the government (i.e., that is included in the cabinet). Moreover, our hypotheses stipulate an interaction effect between these two factors and the quality of a democratic regime, which is measured by the polyarchy index provided by V-Dem. This index quantifies the extent to which the ideal of electoral democracy in its fullest sense is achieved in a given country.[19]

The second set of tests focuses on process-oriented variables that were included in module 1 only. As mentioned earlier in this section, one of the key political factors in citizens' assessment of their democratic institutions relates to their perceptions that politicians know what ordinary citizens' preferences are, that they care about them, and that they take them into account in their public actions. The first factor is neatly measured by the following question

> Some people say that members of [Congress/Parliament] know what ordinary people think. Others say that members of [Congress/Parliament] don't know much about what ordinary people think. Using the scale on this card, (where ONE means that the members of [Congress/Parliament] know what ordinary people think, and FIVE means that the members of [Congress/Parliament] don't know much about what ordinary people think), where would you place yourself?

The second aspect, that is, that politicians care about citizens' preferences, is measured using the following questions: "Some people say that political parties in [country] care what ordinary people think. Others say that political parties in [country] don't care what ordinary people think. Using the scale on this card, (where ONE means that political parties care about what ordinary people think, and FIVE means that they don't care what ordinary people think), where would you place yourself?"

Figure 11 summarizes the distributions of the key independent variables (except for the quality of democracy detailed in Section 1). Variables are rescaled on a 0 to 1 continuum. Although the questions about political parties and politicians could potentially tap the same latent factor, the correlation between respondents' answers to both questions is not very high. That is, the Pearson's r is 0.38, which strongly suggests that they empirically measure different things. Our estimation strategy detailed in Section 2 is making use of a two-level mixed-effects linear model, with individuals nested in elections.

---

[19] See Section 1 for a more detailed discussion about the index.

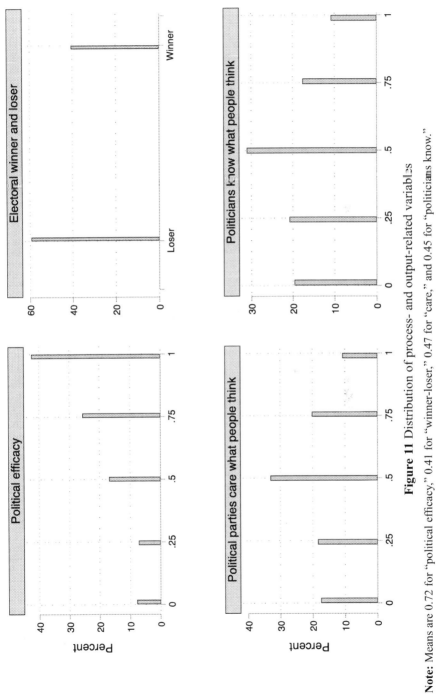

Figure 11 Distribution of process- and output-related variables

Note: Means are 0.72 for "political efficacy," 0.41 for "winner-loser," 0.47 for "care," and 0.45 for "politicians know."

3.4 Findings

3.4.1 Thick and Thin Criterion across Quality of Democracy

The first set of findings compares the importance of a key process-oriented factor (i.e., political efficacy, capturing a general sense of responsiveness), and the most important output-related variable (supporting a winning or a losing party), across the quality of a democracy. The emphasis is thus on the interaction terms of the models. Table 6 shows the regression outputs. Both interaction terms are in the expected direction, and both reach statistical significance at $p < 0.001$. Most importantly, the magnitude of the effect is impressive.

Figure 12 depicts the average marginal effects for each variable of interest across quality of democracy and shows that the two slopes are in the opposite direction. Notably, the effect of political efficacy is not distinct from zero, as it does not reach statistical significance ($p < 0.05$) for values of quality of democracy ranging between 0.15 and 0.40. It increases by a total of 0.15, moving from 0.03 in democracies with the lowest score on the V-Dem's electoral democracy index to 0.12 for countries with democratic institutions of highest quality. Keeping in mind that SWD ranges from 0 to 1, this moderation effect appears as very strong substantially, and neatly supports our expectation that process-oriented considerations are more

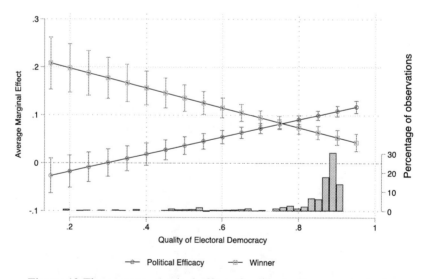

Figure 12 The average marginal effect of political efficacy and winning

Note: Estimations based on Model 1 of Table 6. 95 percent confidence intervals included.

Table 6 Mixed-effects linear regression (DV=satisfaction with democracy)

	Model 1
Electoral democracy index × Political efficacy	0.180***
	(0.028)
Electoral democracy index × Winner	−0.206***
	(0.042)
Political efficacy	−0.054*
	(0.023)
Winner	0.239***
	(0.034)
Electoral democracy index	0.004
	(0.055)
Age (years)	0.000***
	(0.000)
Sex (female=1)	−0.009***
	(0.001)
Education	0.004***
	(0.001)
Income quintiles	0.047***
	(0.002)
GDP per capita (PPP)	0.000***
	(0.000)
Gini	−0.001
	(0.001)
Majoritarian	0.017
	(0.024)
Proportional	−0.031
	(0.021)
Constant	0.285***
	(0.072)
σ^2 elections, political efficacy	−2.888***
	(0.068)
σ^2 elections, intercept	−1.360***
	(0.002)
σ^2 elections, winner	−2.469***
	(0.057)
σ^2 residuals	−2.221***
	(0.054)
N (elections)	192
N (respondents)	199,931

Note: Standard errors in parentheses *$p < 0.05$, **$p < 0.01$, ***$p < 0.001$

important in citizens' assessment of their democratic institutions in high-quality democracies (H1).

Second, we also find strong support for our claim that the importance of output-related considerations should decrease as the quality of a democracy increases (H2). As shown in Figure 12, being on the winning side has a powerful effect of 0.20 in democracies with the lowest score on V-Dem's quality of democracy indicator, and this effect decreases to 0.04 in democracies of the highest quality (for a total difference of 0.16). In other words, the magnitude of the effect of winning is downsized by about five times (that is, 0.20 compared to 0.04), when comparing the highest quality of democracy to the lowest one.

Overall, these moderation effects lead to a typology of democracies with three different scenarios when it comes to understanding citizens' assessment of the democratic institutions in their country. That is, electoral outcomes are much more important than evaluations of the electoral process in democracies of low quality. The weight of these considerations is roughly the same in more established democracies, but not quite close to reaching the "ideal of an electoral democracy." Finally, the effect of citizens' evaluations of the process trumps the impact of being a winner or loser only in democracies of high quality.

3.4.2 Two Process-Oriented Considerations across Quality of Democracy

In the second set of tests, we focus on two process-related considerations known to be key in understanding citizens' SWD (Linz and Stepan 1996a,b; Huang et al. 2008). These factors correspond to the extent to which respondents of module 1 believe that politicians know what ordinary citizens think, as well as how much they believe that political parties care about citizens' preferences. As for the previous section and in line with H1, the key tests consist of interaction effects between these variables and V-Dem's indicator of the quality of a political regime. Moreover, the main output-oriented variable that drives citizens' SWD, that is, whether they voted for a party in government or not, is used as a benchmark. Table 7 shows the main findings.

Both interaction terms (political parties care in Model 1 and politicians know in Model 2) are in the expected (positive) direction and reach statistical significance (at $p < 0.01$). Figure 13 shows the average marginal effects for both variables across quality of democracy. As expected, the process-oriented effects are positive, and the average (direct) effect of perceptions about the extent to which political parties care about citizens' preferences is more important than the perception of whether politicians know what citizens think. The slopes, indicating that the effect varies across context, show that these evaluations become more important in citizens' evaluations of their political institutions

Table 7 Mixed-effect linear regression (DV=satisfaction with democracy)

	Model 1	Model 2
Electoral democracy index × Parties care	0.122[*]	
	(0.061)	
Electoral democracy index × Winner	−0.263[***]	−0.275[***]
	(0.074)	(0.078)
Electoral democracy index × Politicians know		0.167[*]
		(0.072)
Parties care	0.109[*]	
	(0.048)	
Electoral democracy index	0.198[***]	0.197[***]
	(0.057)	(0.056)
Winner	0.259[***]	0.273[***]
	(0.060)	(0.063)
Politicians know		0.014
		(0.057)
Age (years)	0.000[*]	0.000[**]
	(0.000)	(0.000)
Sex (female=1)	−0.011[***]	−0.009[***]
	(0.002)	(0.002)
Education	0.002	0.002
	(0.001)	(0.001)
Income quintiles	0.044[***]	0.047[***]
	(0.004)	(0.004)
GDP per capita (PPP)	0.000[***]	0.000[***]
	(0.000)	(0.000)
Gini	0.004[**]	0.004[**]
	(0.001)	(0.001)
Majoritarian	0.083[***]	0.089[***]
	(0.024)	(0.023)
Proportional	0.072[**]	0.072[**]
	(0.023)	(0.022)
Constant	−1.425[***]	−1.412[***]
	(0.003)	(0.004)
σ^2 elections, intercept	−2.916[***]	−2.686[***]
	(0.148)	(0.142)
σ^2 parties care	−2.782[***]	
	(0.138)	
σ^2 politicians know		−2.722[***]
		(0.137)

Table 7 (cont.)

	Model 1	Model 2
σ^2 winner	-3.079^{***}	-3.115^{***}
	(0.136)	(0.139)
σ^2 residuals	-1.425^{***}	-1.412^{***}
	(0.003)	(0.004)
N (elections)	33	33
N (respondents)	40,936	40,869

Note: Standard errors are in parentheses. Random-effects parameters not shown for the sake of space $^{*}p < 0.05$, $^{**}p < 0.01$, $^{***}p < 0.001$

as the quality of democracy increases. In both cases, the effects are substantially large. For "political parties care" (top panel of Figure 13), the total difference is a little more than 0.08, moving from 0.14 to 0.22. For the "politicians know" (bottom panel), the impact is of 0.10, moving from 0.06 to 0.16. as the quality of a democratic regime increases.

Again, it is worth recalling that the predicted outcome, that is, citizens' SWD, ranges from 0 to 1. Hence, the direct effects of the two variables are not trivial, and, most importantly for our inquiry, this impact greatly differs across contexts. As for political efficacy in the previous section, the impact of these two process-oriented considerations gains importance as the quality of a democracy increases. We thus conclude that our findings strongly support H1.[20]

3.5 Conclusion and Implications

We know that SWD is closely associated with citizens' evaluations of their political systems (electoral process, responsiveness of their government, etc.), as well as the electoral outcomes, particularly related to being on the winning side or not. These considerations are different in nature and relate to distinct features of a political system. We labeled them as either process- or output-oriented considerations. While we know that both sets of factors are crucial in understanding citizens' political support, we still lack a clear characterization of

---

[20] Findings from both sections neatly show that several process-oriented considerations are very important in democracies of high quality, but we are left with little insights about what really matters in low-quality political regimes. Based on Daoust and Nadeau (2021), it is likely that *economic* considerations, not necessarily linked to elections or the electoral process, play a greater role in citizens' evaluations of their democratic institutions in democracies of lower quality.

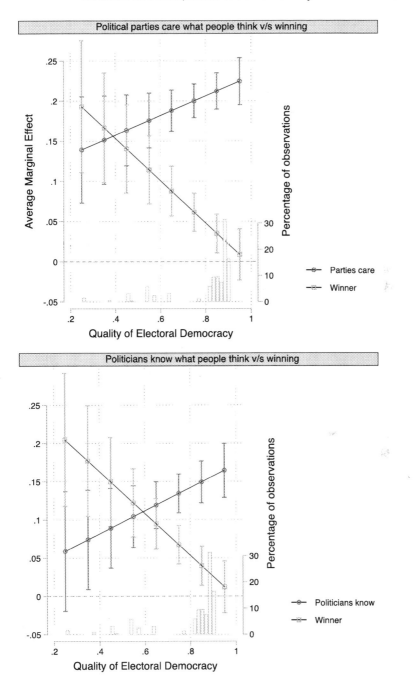

Figure 13 The impact of process- and output-oriented considerations across quality of democracy

Note: Estimations based on Models 1 and 2 of Table 7. 95 percent confidence intervals included.

the conditions under which citizens will prioritize one criterion over the other. In this section, we argue that quality of democracy is the key contextual variable determining the relative weight of process- and output-related factors, which shape citizens' assessments of political institutions.

We leverage data from the CSES database to provide an extensive test of our hypotheses, for which we find clear support. On the one hand, the weight of process-related considerations in citizens' evaluations of how democracy works in their country increases as the quality of a democracy increases. On the other hand, the weight of output-related considerations in citizens' evaluation of how democracy works in their country decreases as the quality of a democracy increases. The effects were all substantially large, to the point that one factor can trump the other based on context. Overall, we hope to have established that the "thin" criterion of being a winner dominates in elected autocracies, whereas more "thick" considerations tapping into a general sense of responsiveness prevail in liberal democracies of higher quality.

Methodologically speaking, our findings show that the average effect of key factors explaining citizens' SWD might be misleading without an integrated context, such as the quality of a democracy. Our work strongly suggests that scholars using large-N comparative datasets should do more to account for differentiated effects of well-known predictors of political support. This applies to current research, but will likely be even more important to consider in future work given that the scope of these datasets (such as the CSES) is continuously increasing.

Our findings also entail important normative implications. First, we should note that relying on the thin criteria of being on the winning side is neither irrational nor frivolous, especially in low-quality democracies. In fact, in contexts where doubts about the fairness of the electoral process are common, it may make sense for an individual to conclude that the victory of their preferred party or candidate is a solid piece of evidence that the democratic system really works. If citizens' assessments are heavily based on such a consideration, however, then this is concerning and underlines the limitations and fragility of their democratic system. Whether citizens mainly rely on their status as a winner or loser to assess their political institutions appears to be a telling indicator of a democracy's vitality. A democratic system rests on a shaky ground when winners perceive elections as fair and losers as forged (Moehler 2009). Citizens who mainly rely on their winner or loser status to assess the performance of their political institutions are sending the worrisome signal that they are prepared to express a high level of satisfaction *only when* they experience positive outcomes and not *when* they face disappointing ones. The manifestation of these attitudes is worrying for the consolidation of democratic regimes, particularly in contexts where "democracy is not the only game in town" (Linz and Stepan, 1996b).

4 Electoral Outcomes, Disputed Legitimacy, and Satisfaction with Democracy

4.1 Introduction

As we have sought to make clear throughout the sections, the "winner–loser gap" is central to the study of citizens' political support, most notably concerning their levels of SWD. Although there is debate about the causes of this gap (Daoust et al. 2023), there exists a general consensus about what it refers to. That is, the gap speaks to the fact that citizens who voted for a party that won the election are systematically more satisfied with the way the democratic regime works in their country than those who voted for a party that lost the election (Curini et al. 2012; Dahlberg and Linde 2016; Martini and Quaranta 2019; Nadeau and Blais 1993). This is arguably one of the most robust relationships in political science.

Despite the centrality of the topic, we still lack insight into key features of this gap. For instance, there is a lack of understanding about the mechanism(s) underlying its occurrence gap. This is, however, rarely acknowledged (and addressed), as most studies tend to take for granted that the cause(s) of the winner–loser gap is known without discussing it. There are two main intuitive (and nonexclusive) explanations for the winner–loser gap. On the one hand, voters might be happy to find the party that they voted for in government, given that they expect them to implement policies that will be beneficial to them. This is a utilitarian argument. On the other hand, voters might be happier when their party wins the election as it simply feels good. No one enjoys defeat; we all prefer winning over losing. This argument is emotionally focused. Both mechanisms are plausible, although relevant literature is unclear about which mechanisms work, and which one(s) would be most important (Best and Seyis 2021; Daoust et al. 2023; Ferland 2021; Toshkov and Mazepus 2020). So far, even the research that has benefited from a clean research design (e.g., Halliez and Thornton 2022) has not managed to isolate the relative importance of both mechanisms.

Another puzzle in the literature relates to how we should conceptualize the notion of "winner" and "loser." Which aspect of party performance matters exactly? Is it about the seat shares, vote shares, or being in government versus in the opposition? To further conceptualize these terms, should measures of party performance be used in absolute terms, that is, from a given election, or in relative terms, that is, evaluated relatively to the performance of a party in the previous election? Theoretically speaking, things are not very straightforward. Many possibilities have been tested (Plescia et al. 2021; Singh et al. 2012), and overall, focusing on whether a party is included in the government after a given election seems to be the best way to capture the winner–loser gap (Anderson et al. 2005; Stiers et al. 2018).

Despite the lack of clarity regarding the mechanism(s) and empirical approach(es) to measuring winners and losers, scholars recognize that the gap is robust to alternative approaches. However, it has been pointed out that its size may be context-dependent. In a pioneering study, Anderson and Guillory (1997) showed that formal institutional settings, leading to more consensual or major-itarian modes of governance, explain part of the cross-country variation in the magnitude of the winner–loser gap. Many scholars have extended this kind of work by looking at other types of contextual features, such as the quality, performance and the length of a democratic regime (Aarts and Thomassen 2008; Dahlberg et al. 2015; Dahlberg and Linde 2016; Martini and Quaranta 2019), the type of election (Singh et al. 2012), and the integrity of the electoral process (Fortin-Rittberger et al. 2017).

In this section, we provide two key sets of results that shed new light on the winner–loser gap. First, we establish more firmly whether the quality of a democracy moderates the size of the winner–loser gap, as there are mixed findings in the literature (Dahlberg and Linde 2016; Martini and Quaranta 2019; Nadeau et al. 2021). Moreover, we examine *who* drives the gap: Is it winners who are benefiting from a boost? Is it losers that are becoming more negative? Or is it both? We address these questions in this section. Second, we aim to deconstruct different electoral statuses beyond the dichotomous view of being in or out of the government and/or having received or not having received a plurality of the popular vote. We pay particular attention to situations that could be potentially challenging for democratic legitimacy, that is, when widely accepted democratic principles clash with the outcome of an election and blur the legitimacy of who should govern. The clearest examples are "electoral inversions" where presidential candidates or political parties benefit from the broadest support among citizens but, due to electoral rules, do not end up governing. We provide an extensive analysis of the winner–loser gap in citi-zens' satisfaction with democracy in contexts of disputed legitimacy.

Our findings show that the depth of the winner–loser gap is a function of the quality of a democracy. That is, the higher the quality of a political regime, the lesser the gap. Moreover, we find that this outcome is driven by *both* winners and losers. As expected, winners win less and losers lose less in high-quality democ-racies where it is clear to everyone that there will be another democratic game to play (under a fair set of rules) only a few years later. Furthermore, this conclusion can be extended through a new typology, which allows us to analyze how the impact of different electoral statuses in the context of disputed legitimacies greatly depends on the quality of a democratic regime. The results show that the convergence in levels of SWD between winners and losers in high-quality democracies is also observed when we use a more refined typology of electoral outcomes that considers, both, the level of support a party receives and its participation in government. This result re-emphasizes the finding that voters in established democracies are less sensitive to electoral outcomes than citizens in emerging democracies, even in context of electoral inversions. Methodologically speaking, our results send a note of caution to scholars who average the effect of winning (or losing) when analyzing the winner–loser gap. Normatively speaking, our findings further reinforce the idea that a small gap is a characteristic of a healthy and well-established democratic regime and that the role of the quality of democracy in moderating the gap (in the context of disputed legitimacy or not) does not exclusively operate through its effect on losers.

4.2 The Aftermath of Elections, Citizens' Reactions, and Contested Legitimacy across Contexts

4.2.1 The Meaning of Winning and Losing across Contexts

It is widely acknowledged that the winner–loser gap is important for democracy, but the literature has focused more on losers than winners. Book titles like *Losers' Consent: Elections and Democratic Legitimacy* (Anderson et al. 2005) or article titles, such as "Accepting the election outcome: the effect of participation on losers' consent" (Nadeau and Blais 1993), highlight this unbalanced focus. It is understandable that, intuitively, scholars are preoccupied with losers' reactions: After all, they are the ones that are much more likely to be disappointed by the current rules of the game and challenge democratic stability. However, a consequence of this focus is that some features that apply to both winners and losers have been overlooked.

The information environment, among others, should impact all voters in their reactions to and interpretations of the electoral outcome. Moreover, they are likely all prompted by motivated reasoning, which suggests that voters (both winners and losers) will be exposed to different evidence that can comfort or challenge their evaluations of the electoral process (e.g., fairness, integrity) and the legitimacy of the electoral outcome (Kernell and Mullinix 2019; Lodge and Taber 2013; Redlawsk et al. 2010). Moreover, the information environment affects what is salient or not in citizens' evaluations of political objects (Christmann 2018; Daoust and Nadeau 2021; Rohrschneider and Loveless 2010). Examples were given in the previous section, where we found evidence that the weight of process- and output-related considerations in citizens' evaluations of how their democracy works in practice varies across contexts. That is, process-focused considerations were more important in democracies of higher quality, while output-related considerations were more significant in democracies of lower quality. Overall, research on the role of the information environment and motivated reasoning suggests that the quality of a democracy will affect what considerations are salient in citizens' minds and that voters will likely be exposed to evidence that confirms their prior beliefs about an electoral outcome's legitimacy. This could be damaging if there is a popular discourse challenging the electoral process and outcome.

Second, winners' and losers' SWD should also be affected by the fact that elected governments are more likely to ensure the hold of (fair) elections after their legal term, which allows opposition parties to have an adequate opportunity to convince voters. The straightforward implication is that there is, overall, simply much less at stake: in high-quality democracy, winners win less and losers lose less. There is less to win and less to lose because there will be, regardless of the outcome, another fair game in a few years. Hence, the quality of a democratic regime should moderate the size of the winner–loser gap, by reducing the effect of both winning and losing. Overall, combined with the literature on the information environment and motivated reasoning, we expect that, in high-quality democracies, the positive impact of winning and the negative effect of losing would both be reduced. In other words, we hypothesize that in high-quality democracies, winners win less and losers lose less compared to low-quality democratic regimes.

This expectation is also consistent with the influential work of Przeworski (1991), who suggests that democracy is "self-reinforcing." For Przeworski (2008), a key role of elections is to designate "winners" and "losers," and this designation "is an instruction to the participants as to what they should and should not do" (p. 1). "Democracy," still following the author, "is in equilibrium when winners and losers obey the inherent instructions in their designation." Przeworski (2008: 1) For all the reasons presented so far, it seems reasonable to argue that the narrowing gap between losers and winners in established democracies (that winners would win less while losers would lose less) will make it easier for both groups (and particularly for the losers) to accept the "designations" from the electoral outcome, thus helping to ensure the stability of the democratic system.

4.2.2 Winning and Losing: An Extended Typology

The idea that the power of political parties or candidates should be roughly proportional to their share of support among the population (measured by vote share at the national level) is rather intuitive, as the contrary would arguably be unfair (Karp and Banducci 2008; Lijphart 1999; Plescia et al. 2020). This is important because, similar to what we observed in Section 2, perceptions of fairness of the electoral outcomes can affect citizens' attitudes toward their democratic institutions (Miller 2001). In other words, the proportionality between the support that a party receives and its power (usually measured in number of seats) is taken as an indicator of the fairness of electoral outcomes. In a recent and insightful study, Plescia et al. (2020) showed that "citizens do care about how votes are converted into seats" and that "disproportionality decreases support for the voting rules for both large and small parties' voters." (p. 746). In this section, we do not examine the link between proportionality and citizens' SWD, but we focus on a context where there is an imbalance in the power of the party based on their support among citizens. These situations lead to a disputed legitimacy that can impact citizens' evaluations of their democratic institutions.

The first scenario refers to "electoral inversions." Geruso et al. (2022) describe electoral inversions as a situation where "the popular vote winner loses the election" (p. 327) – see also Felsenthal and Miller (2015: 173).[21] Linked to proportionality, it is reasonable to expect that citizens who voted for the party receiving the most votes (i.e., the party benefiting from the largest support among the population compared to all other parties) believe that their party should lead the government formation. Electoral inversions, which result in a "reversed legitimacy," can be problematic for citizens' democratic support given that some voters might perceive this situation as incongruent with democratic principles. This is also the case among scholars, as encapsulated by Cervas and Grofman (2019) that "many political scientists hold the popular vote principle to be sacrosanct." (p. 1325). Moreover, Kurrild-Klitgaard (2013) refers to electoral inversions as "voting paradoxes."

The second scenario is the mirror situation of an electoral inversion, that is, the inclusion of a party that did not win the popular vote in the government. Such a party is usually treated as a junior coalition partner of a multi-party government. Yet, voters supporting such a party should not be as satisfied with democracy as those voters of the party who won the popular vote and made it into government. This scenario is likely if these partisans believe that the vote for their preferred party was not properly tallied in the first place, or if they think that, because of suspicious backdoor negotiations, it did not get its fair share of portfolios. Based on the literature reviewed in the previous sections (especially Section 3), there are good reasons to believe that these perceptions are more widespread in less established democracies.

In brief, dissatisfaction with the functioning of democratic institutions is driven by the translation of the vote into parliamentary representation or government. In this context, it can be argued that the voters of the winning party in terms of vote-share can be at least partially satisfied with a system that

---

[21] It is worth noting that, in this case, the phrase "loses the election" means not making it into government, which reinforces the view that winning or losing is about the government/opposition dichotomy (Anderson et al. 2005; Stiers et al. 2018).

recognizes the electoral strength of their party. Indeed, this "first party" status is often claimed by political parties, regardless of whether or not they are in government. In the past, this was seen with the Communists in France (Fauvet 1964). The case for voters whose preferred party is defeated at the polls but still included in the governing coalition is different. These voters may be satisfied with being in government but nonetheless believe that votes for their preferred candidate were not adequately counted, or that their candidate did not get its fair share of power in the government. For these reasons, it is possible to believe that the level of satisfaction with democratic institutions of voters in these more ambiguous situations may fall somewhere between the levels observed among those who won outright (i.e., their party received the most votes and is in government) or lost outright (i.e., their preferred party did not receive the most votes and is not in government). It is also plausible to think that the differences between the levels of satisfaction among these four groups will be more pronounced in emerging democracies than in established democracies.

Scenarios where the legitimacy of the different political parties is disputed are not uncommon. Moreover, these scenarios are not constrained to specific electoral systems or features of a democracy. Indeed, they can arise in a variety of contexts, which makes them quite common. As shown in the next section, more than 15 percent of citizens surveyed in the CSES voted for a party that either won the popular vote but did not make it into government formation (about 4 percent), or made it into government without having won the popular vote (about 11 percent). Despite the frequency of these scenarios as well as their possibility of posing problems for democratic support, the contexts and effects on political support are understudied.

One of the most relevant studies on disputed legitimacy is the recent piece by Carey et al. (2021). The authors directly examine the impact of electoral inversions and reversed legitimacy on citizens' democratic support. Using a survey experiment and fictive scenarios (where the vote shares of the US presidential candidates as well as the Electoral College results are manipulated), the authors find that electoral inversions negatively affect the legitimacy of the winner. Moreover, the margin of victory (1 percent, 3 percent, or 5 percent) does not seem to matter. Instead, what matters is whether the winner of the vote makes it to government. Halliez and Thornton (2022) also investigate electoral inversions and democratic support, yet their main focus is on unclear electoral outcomes. The authors leverage panel data from the ANES of the 2000 US election (and the 2002 follow-up), when Al Gore won the popular vote but lost the presidential contest (through the Electoral College) to George W. Bush. Findings show that there was no difference in Republican and Democrat voters' levels of SWD in 2000 (before the outcome was known), but a substantial gap emerged in 2002 (after the outcome was known).

These two studies (Carey et al. 2021; Halliez and Thornton 2022) are insightful. However, while one is based on a fictive vignette instead of a real-world scenario, both focus on a single (particular) case study, the United States. This section analyzes disputed legitimacy and democratic attitudes using a greater amount and variety of real-world electoral outcomes, rendering this the first comparative analysis of this kind. In the following section, we outline the data and indicators that we will use for this exploration.

4.3 Data and Indicators

For this analysis, we use all five modules from the CSES described in Section 1. Overall, it includes data from more than 200 elections from fifty-seven countries between 1996 and 2020. This section is centered around the electoral status and the winner–loser gap. As mentioned, there are many indicators of party performance that are all, to some degree, insightful (e.g., see Plescia et al. 2021). In line with conventional wisdom and notably the work by Stiers et al. (2018; see also Anderson et al. 2005), we code winners as voters who supported a party that makes it to government (i.e., has at least one member among the cabinet) while losers are those who supported a party that ends up in the opposition (see Section 2).

Most research on the winner–loser gap work focuses on winning versus losing. In other words, it provides a single estimate of the impact of the winner–loser gap. Here, we compare the average marginal effect of voting for a winning party, as well as the impact of voting for a losing party compared to not having voted (i.e., abstainers) on SWD. Doing so allows us to analyze who, among voters, are responsible for the expected moderation effect from the quality of a democracy on the size of the winner–loser gap. The first question used to generate this three-category variable taps into whether respondents voted or abstained in the election. Self-reported measures of voter turnout have often led to an overestimation of respondents who claimed to have voted (Selb and Munzert 2013), but research does not find that this has substantial implications for statistical inference (Achen and Blais 2016; Blais and Daoust 2020; Morin-Chassé et al. 2017). For those who said they have voted, we used the vote choice questions to find which party they voted for. This is used to match respondents' vote choice to a party that ended up in government (i.e., winner) or in the opposition (i.e., loser). Overall, 41.6 percent are coded as winners, 41.6 percent as losers, and 16.8 percent as abstainers.[22]

---

[22] The CSES, like most surveys, underestimates the proportion of abstainers (McAllister and Quinlan 2022). That said, this bias should not affect our statistical inferences when we examine the impact of an independent variable as Achen and Blais (2016) have demonstrated that using a validated measure of voter turnout or a self-reported question that underestimate abstainers lead to the same conclusions (see also Dassonneville and Hooghe 2017).

For the second set of results of this section, we unpack the traditional typology around winning and losing by including mixed outcomes, such as where the legitimacy of the elected government is more ambiguous compared to a clear victory or a clear loss for the party that a voter supported. As outlined earlier, this refers to a situation where a party won the popular vote but was excluded from the government, or where a party makes it to the cabinet without having won the popular vote. We thus generated a dichotomous variable identifying whether the party won the most votes or not. In addition to the party performance variable that focused on whether or not the party made it to the government or not, this variable allowed us to generate a five-category variable. The categories are as follows: the respondent's party is included in the government and won the popular vote (win/win), they supported a party that is included in the government without having won the popular vote (win/lose), they voted for a party that did not make it to the government despite having won the popular vote (lose/win), they supported a party that lost the popular vote and is not included in government (lost/lost), or they abstained from voting. These categories respectively represent about 28 percent, 14 percent, 4 percent, 38 percent, and 17 percent of the CSES' respondents.

The third key variable used in this section is the quality of a democratic regime. As for previous sections, we make use of V-Dem's polyarchy index. It quantifies the extent to which the ideal of electoral democracy in its fullest sense is achieved in a given country (see Section 1). Our estimation strategy is also the same as described in previous sections. That is, we rely on mixed-effects linear models predicting SWD, recoded on a 0 to 1 scale.

4.4 Results

4.4.1 The Winner–Loser Gap across Quality of Democracy

Our findings replicate the approach and results of Nadeau et al. (2021) but with an updated version of the dataset thanks to the inclusion of the latest module of the CSES. For reasons described in Section 4.3, we deviate from the conventional approach in estimating the effect of winning or losing an election by using a categorical variable where voting for a party that makes it to the government, as well as voting for a party that ends up in the opposition, are compared to citizens who abstained. Following an examination of the moderation effect of quality of democracy on the winner–loser gap, the key advantage of this approach is that it allows us to examine who, among winners and losers, drives this relationship. Table 8 shows the regression output.

We expect both moderation effects to indicate that the impact of winning and losing moves closer to zero as the quality of a democratic regime increases.

Table 8 Winners and losers compared to abstainers, across quality of democracy

	Model 1
Electoral democracy index × Loser	0.122***
	(0.030)
Electoral democracy index × Winner	−0.094**
	(0.034)
Loser (ref=abstainer)	−0.081***
	(0.025)
Winner (ref=abstainer)	0.167***
	(0.028)
Electoral democracy index	0.048
	(0.049)
Age (years)	0.000***
	(0.000)
Sex (female=1)	−0.009***
	(0.001)
Income quintiles	0.051***
	(0.002)
Education	0.005***
	(0.001)
GDP per capita (PPP)	0.000***
	(0.000)
Gini	0.001
	(0.001)
Majoritarian	0.047*
	(0.022)
Proportional	−0.001
	(0.019)
Constant	0.185**
	(0.064)
σ^2 elections, intercept	−2.730***
	(0.063)
σ^2 winner	−2.904***
	(0.068)
σ^2 loser	−2.327***
	(0.053)
σ^2 residuals	−1.348***
	(0.002)
N (elections)	196
N (respondents)	214,005

Note: Standard errors in parentheses $^{*}p < 0.05$, $^{**}p < 0.01$, $^{***}p < 0.001$

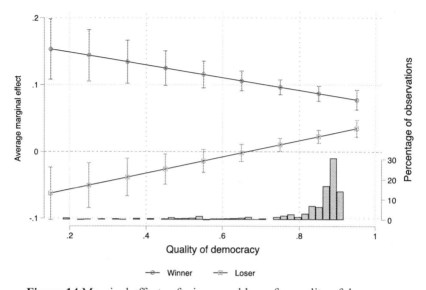

Figure 14 Marginal effects of winner and loser for quality of democracy

Note: The reference category is abstainer. Estimations based on Table 8 with 95 percent confidence intervals included.

Given that the effect of winning is positive in low-quality contexts but negative for losers, we should expect a negative interaction term for winners and a positive interaction term for losers. In Table 9, we can see that both interaction terms are in the expected directions. This suggests that winners win "less" and that losers lose "less" in democracies of better quality. To grasp the substantial effect of this relationship, we plot the average marginal effect for winners (compared to abstainers) and losers (compared to abstainers) in Figure 14.

Being a loser is associated with a negative effect of −0.06 in low-quality democracies (compared to abstainers). This effect becomes indistinguishable from abstainers in democracies with a quality score around 0.5, while voting for a losing party becomes associated with a positive effect of 0.03 (again, compared to abstainers) in the most established democracies. The total effect is thus almost 0.10. The moderation effect on winners is more straightforward: it is always positive, but its effect decreases by 0.07, moving from about 0.15 to 0.08. as the quality of democracy increases. Both interaction effects reach $p < 0.01$, as shown in Table 8. Overall, the gap in the effect between winning and losing across the quality of a democracy varies very substantially. At the lowest score on the x-axis, the gap is about 0.21 (−0.06 for losers and almost +0.15 for winners), whereas, at the highest level, the gap is less than 0.05 (+0.03 for losers and +0.08 for winners; to get a sense of the predicted levels of SWD, see Figure D.1 of the Online Appendix).

Table 9 An extended typology of electoral outcomes

	Model 1
Electoral democracy index × Win/Win	−0.126**
	(0.039)
Electoral democracy index × Win/Lose	0.033
	(0.039)
Electoral democracy index × Lose/Win	0.160
	(0.089)
Electoral democracy index × Lose/Lose	0.117***
	(0.029)
Win/Win (ref=abstainers)	0.200***
	(0.032)
Win/Lose (ref=abstainers)	0.043
	(0.032)
Lose/Win (ref=abstainers)	−0.090
	(0.073)
Lose/Lose (ref=abstainers)	−0.079***
	(0.024)
Electoral democracy index	0.055
	(0.051)
Age (years)	0.000***
	(0.000)
Sex (female=1)	−0.009***
	(0.001)
Income quintiles	0.049***
	(0.002)
Education	0.005***
	(0.001)
GDP per capita (PPP)	0.000***
	(0.000)
Gini	0.001
	(0.001)
Majoritarian	0.046*
	(0.022)
Proportional	−0.002
	(0.019)
Constant	0.179**
	(0.067)
σ^2 elections, intercept	−2.653***
	(0.067)

Table 9 (cont.)

	Model 1
σ^2 Win/Win	−3.013[***]
	(0.098)
σ^2 Win/Lose	−2.740[***]
	(0.155)
σ^2 Lose/Win	−2.949[***]
	(0.069)
σ^2 Lose/Lose	−2.327[***]
	(0.053)
σ^2 Residuals	−2.327[***]
	(0.053)
N (elections)	195
N (respondents)	213,195

Note: Standard errors are in parentheses. Random-effects parameters are not shown.
[*] $p < 0.05$, [**] $p < 0.01$, [***] $p < 0.001$

Altogether, Figure 14 highlights two key findings. Firstly, we can conclude that the winner–loser gap is a function of the quality of a democratic regime. That is, the gap is reduced in magnitude as quality increases. Second, this reduction in the size of the gap is due to both winners and losers, moving by about 0.07 and 0.10, respectively. The results are similar to the ones obtained by Nadeau et al. (2021), although the additional thirty-three elections slightly reduced the moderation effect for winners.

4.4.2 Mixed Outcomes, Disputed Legitimacy, and Context

The winner–loser gap is centered around whether a party or candidate makes it to the government or not (Anderson et al. 2005; Anderson and LoTempio 2002; Stiers et al. 2018). However, as described previously, there can be disputed legitimacy in a wide variety of contexts (e.g., in majoritarian and proportional representation electoral systems, democracies of high or low quality). To get a better sense of the effect of electoral inversions and reversed legitimacy, we estimate the effects of having voted for a party that makes it to the government (or not) as well as having won the popular vote (or not) – compared to abstaining. Given that we have good reasons to believe that the impact of these mixed results may vary between emergent and established democracies, we also include a series of interactive terms in the model to assess the likely

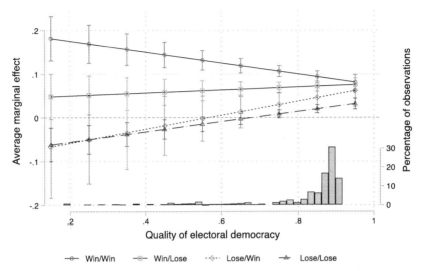

Figure 15 Average marginal effect of electoral status across quality of democracy

Note: Based on Table 9, 95 percent confidence intervals included.

moderation effect of the quality of democracy on the relationship between these various electoral outcomes and citizens' SWD.

Table 9 shows the regression outputs predicting citizens' SWD. The key findings are shown by the interaction terms between electoral status and quality of democracy (using V-Dem's indicator). As seen in Figure 15, we used these coefficients to plot the average marginal effects, all compared to abstainers. In line with the findings from the previous section, we find that the winner–loser gap is a function of the quality of a democracy. Furthermore, using this new typology of different electoral statuses has led to the interaction term for clear winners (win/win) to become statistically significant and have an interaction effect as strong as that for clear losers (coefficient of about 0.13 for the former and 0.12 for the latter). This contrasts with the previous sections where the loser effect was (slightly) greater.

The effect of the lose/win category – voting for a party that was excluded from the government despite having won the popular vote – is also note-worthy. These cases of electoral inversion are associated with a negative effect on citizens' satisfaction with democracy in low-quality democracies. However, as the quality of a democratic regime increases, this situation is associated with greater levels of SWD (compared to abstainers), with an average marginal effect of about 0.05. Hence, the potential negative effects of electoral inversions seem to be much more salient in low-quality democracies. Thus, whether clear (win/win or lose/lose) or more ambiguous, the results neatly indicate that the effect of citizens' electoral status on their level of SWD varies greatly according to the quality of democracy. The gap in levels of SWD among these groups, clearly apparent in low-quality democracies (0.18, 0.05, −0.07, −.006 for the win/win, win/lose, lose/win and lose/lose categories, respectively), almost disappears in established democracies (0.08, 0.07, 0.06, and 0.03 for the same groups).

4.5 Conclusion

The winner–loser gap in political support is vastly studied and considered important for numerous reasons. Normatively speaking, the extent to which citizens are satisfied with their democratic institutions and express a strong commitment to democracy should not heavily depend on whether they win a free and fair election. President Joe Biden neatly encapsulated this idea in the following statement after a year of riots on the capitol, which constituted a direct challenge to democracy: "You can't love your country only when you win. You can't obey the law only when it's convenient."

While some studies examined whether the quality of a democratic regime moderates the magnitude of the winner–loser gap (Dahlberg and Linde 2016; Martini and Quaranta 2019; Nadeau et al. 2021), we provide what is, to our knowledge, the most extensive evidence that this is indeed the case. As the quality of a democracy increases, the size of the gap decreases.

We also examined a potentially problematic situation where electoral outcomes clash with intuitively and widely accepted democratic principles. These contexts lead to disputed legitimacy. Our findings show that disputed legitimacies do not seem to produce massively dissatisfied citizens in established democracies. However, things are not as clear in emergent democracies. Overall, we believe that we should focus at least as much on abstainers as on losers – keeping in mind that abstainers display lower levels of satisfaction with their democratic institutions.

Finally, it is also interesting to note that for both sets of conclusions and implications, the United States are clear outliers. First, the winner–loser gap should be among the smallest given that the country is said to be a high-quality democracy. This is, however, not what research suggests (Enders and Thornton 2021; Norris 2019). Second, the US-based study from Carey et al. (2021) on electoral inversions suggested that citizens' democratic attitudes in a context of reversed legitimacy were quite substantially affected, an outcome that may perhaps signal another instance of the US "exceptionalism."

5 Conclusion, Implications, and Further Research

Satisfaction with democracy is vastly studied in social sciences, and there are good reasons for this interest (see Section 1). The assumption that liberal democracy represents the best form of governance calls for research to improve our understanding of how citizens evaluate their political institutions. This is especially of interest across different regimes, as they vary based on the extent to which they achieve this ideal democratic regime. So far, more than 2,500 articles have been published with the aim of contributing to our knowledge of citizens' levels of SWD (Valgarðsson and Devine 2021: note 1).

Most of the research on SWD has focused on the direct effects of individual factors (sociodemographics, attitudes and values, political behaviors, etc.) and macro-level variables (electoral systems, economic development, etc.) on citizens' evaluations of the functioning of their political institutions (Dassonneville and McAllister 2020; Farrell and McAllister 2006; Ferland 2021; Han and Chang 2016). The contribution of this Element belongs to a stream of research that examines how the different political contexts across countries shape the strength of key determinants of SWD. This type of research is not, of course, an uncharted territory. For instance, Anderson and Guillory's (1997) pioneered work using data from eleven Western European countries showed that citizens' post-electoral assessments of their democratic institutions vary across political institutions (measured by a consensus-majoritarian index). However, we believe that our Element further contributes to this field for two key reasons.

First, we have advanced our understanding in this area through the scope and variety of the data used. Our data were obtained from the CSES, which is a comprehensive and rich database. As a result, the scope of our empirical demonstration is based on roughly 200 elections that were held in a large variety of national contexts and which cover a time span of a quarter of a century (1996–2020).[23] This Element thus upholds the belief that political scientists must take advantage of the increased availability of rich comparative data across time and space. This allows us to rigorously analyze the effects of the political context and elections on the determinants of citizens' satisfaction with the functioning of their democratic institutions.

Second, this Element further contributes to the field through its central focus on the relationship between elections and SWD. More specifically, and perhaps more importantly, we have relied on fundamental and traditional studies in

---

[23] Although we leveraged the post-electoral survey data from the Comparative Study of Electoral Systems throughout this book, other comparative datasets, such as the World Values Survey, can be very useful to study political support depending on one's objectives. Our findings and implications regarding the integration of contexts apply to all these comparative inquiries.

political science about the relationship between the electoral process and the nature and functioning of democratic institutions. For instance, previous scholarly works, taken as classics in the field, show the duality of the electoral process (Dahl, Duverger, Easton, Lipset, Norris, etc.). This work has put forward the claim that elections can be both conflictual and consensual. On the one hand, it may be conflictual because opposing views are expressed and debated, which leads to a division in society between winners and losers. On the other hand, elections may also be consensual because they constitute a peaceful mechanism for resolving collective debates on broad legitimacy.

This distinction is central throughout this Element. In particular, it has allowed us to demonstrate why and how the effects of this duality manifest themselves differently in established and emerging democracies. To be sure, the vast majority of citizens of low- and high-quality democracies share the belief that free and fair elections are an essential indicator of well-functioning democratic institutions (Dalton et al. 2007; see also Section 1). However, our findings showed that, among other things, winning and losing seem to mean and be attributed to different things across varying qualities of democracies. In emerging democracies, defeat is interpreted by many as a signal that fraud and manipulation may have tainted the electoral process. Moreover, this reaction also reflects a sense among these same losers that they may be left behind by the newly elected government, since the same factors that would have favored its dubious election – the absence of an independent media, lack of fairness in how the other party or candidates plays the democratic game, and so on – will limit its responsiveness to the needs of voters who did not support it. Winners in low-quality democracies, on the other hand, are more likely to believe that the electoral process was fair and, therefore, that the policies of the elected government, which will favor their voters, are legitimate. This gap between winners and losers is much less pronounced in established democracies (see in particular Section 4), where both groups tend to recognize the fairness of the electoral process (see Section 2) and, therefore, do not interpret the winner's victory as a blank check to systematically favor the groups that supported them. The preceding lines show that the meaning attached by citizens to the conduct of elections, the outcomes, and the anticipated consequences varies considerably according to the quality of democracy.

In the next section, we review the results of the sections, where each contributed to our understanding of the relationship between the electoral process and outcomes on SWD across contexts. We then provide a conclusion that includes normative implications, notably for our understanding of the winner–loser gap and how it relates to the degree of a democratic regime's maturity. Finally, we outline a fruitful avenue for future research.

5.1 Lessons about Elections and Satisfaction with Democracy

The main results of this Element focused on an indicator measuring citizens' SWD. The importance of this measure in all of our analyses required that we present the scope and limitations of this indicator. This was done in Section 1, which discussed what the indicator does and does not capture, and provided very reassuring tests regarding the reliability and comparability of the measurement. Like other scholars, we concluded that asking respondents how satisfied or unsatisfied they are with the functioning of democracy in their country is a good measure of how they assess the performance of their democratic institutions *in practice*. In other words, following the distinction from Easton (1965), we tapped a measure of specific political support (versus diffuse support). Moreover, the tests provided in Section 1 showed that these assessments have similar meanings across countries and can therefore be used to undertake a comparative analysis over time and space of citizens' satisfactions with the functioning of democracy. Finally, we noted that the levels of SWD (as well as the mean quality of democracy) from the CSES data are remarkably stable over time (from 1996 to 2020), and that this stability is not due to the differences in countries included in the modules throughout the years.

Section 2 examined what many citizens and experts consider to be the cornerstone of democracy, namely the holding of fair elections. To this end, we first focused on data from module 1 of the CSES, which include an indicator that directly measures citizens' perceptions of the degree of fairness characterizing the election held in a given country. We then analyzed the determinants of these perceptions and captured the extent to which they were linked to citizens' SWD. Moreover, we cross-referenced the data from the five CSES modules with information from the National Elections across Democracy and Autocracy Dataset project (Hyde and Marinov 2012, 2019) in order to assess how the presence of international observers might affect citizens' evaluations of their democratic institutions. We uncovered a positive effect of electoral monitoring in emerging democracies, which is reassuring.

These results provided us with important insights. First, they showed that citizens' perceptions of the fairness of the electoral process are grounded in reality – they are strongly related to the degree of a democratic institution's development in a given country. The results not only showed that these evaluations are strongly related to SWD, which is expected, but also demonstrated that they are very strongly linked to the status of winners or losers in emerging democracies. This is worrisome, since the stability of democracies depends on the recognition of the legitimacy of the electoral process, especially by the losers. It is this difficulty, referred to as the "information problem," which the practice of election monitoring seeks to address, as it aims to reassure all voters about the integrity of the electoral process and outcomes. Our analyses suggested that this objective seems to be at least partially met insofar as it is possible to observe a positive effect between the presence of election observers and the level of satisfaction with democracy in emerging democracies.

Section 3 leveraged all five modules of the CSES to unpack the relevance of different criteria used by citizens when assessing the performance of their democracy, and to examine whether these vary across the quality of the democratic institutions. On the one hand, findings neatly showed that citizens' evaluations are much more *output-oriented* in emerging democracies. This can be explained by the strong link between a respondent's status as winner or loser, and their SWD in emerging democracies. This effect almost vanished in established democracies. On the other hand, we were also able to show that citizens in established democracies evaluated the performance of their democratic institutions less on the basis of the one-time outcome of a particular election, and instead put more emphasis on *process-oriented* considerations. That is, they relied more heavily on broader perceptions of the democratic process, namely that elections produce responsive governments, that politicians have a good sense of what citizens want, and that they care about these preferences and demands. These two findings are fundamental because they reinforce and deepen a central idea in political science that elections mark a high point in democratic life. In established democracies, elections resemble such a political moment. However, our findings suggested that elections in emerging democracies are more than a high point: they are, unfortunately, an event against which the broader democratic process is assessed, leading to a very large winner–loser gap.

Section 4 capitalized on this opposition between losers and winners by showing that, contrary to what has long been suggested (Anderson et al. 2005; Nadeau and Blais 1993), the decline of the winner–loser gap in the level of SWD is not exclusively due to the post-election reactions of the losers. In fact, the results showed that more than the rallying of losers, it is the convergence of *both* winners and losers following an election that seems to characterize the post-election context in established democracies. Moreover, this convergence was observed even when we used a different typology, such as one that contrasts clear outcomes (i.e., lose the popular vote and is not included in the government) to more ambiguous ones, which can lead to a disputed legitimacy context (i.e., electoral inversions where the most popular party or candidate does not make it to the government). This result is fundamental in that it shows that both winners and losers do not appear to attach undue importance to the holding of a particular election in their assessments of the performance of their democratic institutions. In brief, citizens' assessments of their democratic institutions through the lenses of elections seem to be more "single-shot" (output-oriented) in emergent democracies and more of a "continuous-shooting" type (process-oriented) in established democracies.

5.2 Conclusion and Further Research

This Element provided an extensive analysis of elections and SWD. More precisely, we examined electoral outcomes and processes, and integrated context (focusing on quality of democracy) to analyze how it shapes key determinants of satisfaction with democracy. The analyses, which covered nearly 200 elections from 1996–2020, lead to some major conclusions, some of which may seem paradoxical at first glance. The results showed that citizens' perceptions of the fairness of the electoral process are rooted in reality and have a decisive influence on their evaluations of the performance of their democratic institutions. These perceptions are, however, strongly colored by respondents' electoral status (i.e., winner or losers), particularly in emerging democracies. The finding points to the challenge in establishing a lasting bond of trust between citizens and the electoral process in this context. However, the positive effect of election monitoring on SWD in emerging democracies is an encouraging result. It serves as a strong reminder of the need to continue investing in appropriate resources in order to build trust in emerging democracies.

The results also showed that the political determinants (output-oriented and process-oriented) with the greatest impact on citizens' assessments of the performance of democratic institutions varied substantially across qualities of democracy. Citizens of emerging democracies seemed to be very sensitive to their electoral status. In contrast, citizens in established democracies seemed to base their evaluation on wider perceptions of the processes tapping whether elected officials are responsive to their needs rather than a particular output. The meaning and scope of elections thus appeared to differ greatly depending on the context. It is certainly not wrong to say that elections resemble an important moment in citizens' democratic practices, and to call it a high point in political and civic life in established societies is not out-of-bounds. However, this does not seem to be commensurate with the importance of elections in emerging democracies, where electoral outcomes are more important than election processes in grasping citizens' SWD.

The findings further showed that the effect of holding elections does not seem to have a very strong impact on citizens' degree of SWD in high-quality democracies despite the fact that some end up on the winning side while others lose the election. This result may seem surprising and contradictory, as it is common to think that the holding of a free and competitive election provides evidence of the proper functioning of democratic institutions in a country. However, this paradox may instead be an eloquent demonstration that a democracy is well established and functioning as it should be. Furthermore, it seems reasonable for citizens to not attach undue influence on the most recent election when determining their SWD. Firstly, the vast majority of citizens in a democracy (winners and losers alike) share the belief that the election was conducted fairly. Secondly, there is also the shared belief that a singular election is just one link in a trajectory of elections that were held under the same (fair and legitimate) conditions in the past, and that will be conducted in the same manner in the future. In fact, it could be argued that this small effect reflects both the health and maturity of a democracy. Normatively speaking, we believe that a smaller gap in citizens' political support is desirable.

Overall, we hope to have demonstrated the importance of context in understanding citizens' SWD. Nonetheless, we also acknowledge that there is more to be done (see Singh and Mayne 2023). Whilst the quality of a democracy is key, as shown throughout this Element, we believe that worldwide trends of decentralization provide a fruitful avenue for future research. In every part of the world, subnational governments are becoming more important and citizens therefore also attribute greater importance to these levels of governance (Daoust and Blais 2021; Golder et al. 2017; Lago 2021; Schakel and Romanova 2018). Who governs at the subnational level, i.e., who can make use of the new/increasing powers, are determined by elections? Do electoral process and outcomes affect citizens at all? If so, is the influence similar to what we saw in national elections? We know very little about these questions. We currently lack systematic work on whether and how different levels of government (i.e., local, regional, national, supranational) and their respective elections influence citizens' assessment of the function of their democratic institutions. Moreover, the study of political support and how it is shaped (or not) by different levels of elections is underdeveloped compared to other topics. This is odd given its importance.[24] As for our inquiry throughout this Element, we believe that such work is important, and will very likely continue to gain traction in the near future.

Finally, we also hope that our work underscores the critical importance of using large comparative studies in the ongoing efforts to better understand the relationship between elections and citizens' views of democracy across time and space. For example, comprehensive and rich datasets are crucial to studying

---

[24] For example, research on voter turnout or electoral accountability is already characterized by some debates on the extent to which context affects citizens (e.g., Daoust and Blais 2021).

citizens' vote choice, which are directly linked to elections – for recent examples using CSES data, see Otjes and Stiers (2021), Daoust et al. 2021 or Jungkunz et al. (2021). We should note that our study also contributes to improving our understanding of other topics for which SWD is a key predictor. Indeed, scholars have demonstrated that "dissatisfied democrats" are more passive and likely to support radical and/or populist parties (Bélanger and Aarts 2006; Hansen and Olsen 2019) and that sustained dissatisfaction with the performance of the democratic system may have the potential to engender spirals of political distrust and discontent (Hooghe and Dassonneville 2018; Rooduijn et al. 2016). Therefore, better knowledge on the link between elections and satisfaction with democracy seems an appropriate place to start in order to avoid these spirals

References

Aarts, K. and Thomassen, J., 2008. "Satisfaction with Democracy: Do Institutions Matter?" *Electoral Studies* 27(1): 5–18.

Achen, C. and Blais, A., 2016. "Intention to Vote, Reported Vote, and Validated Vote." In Johan, A. E. and Farrell, D. M. (eds), *The Act of Voting: Identities, Institutions and Locale.* London: Routledge, pp. 195–215.

Alemika, E. E., 2007. "Quality of Elections, Satisfaction with Democracy and Political Trust in Africa." Afrobarometer Working Paper No. 84. www .afrobarometer.org/files/documents/working_paper/AfropaperNo84.pdf (May 15, 2015).

Alvarez, R. M., Adams-Cohen, N., Kim, S. Y. S., and Li, Y., 2020. *Securing American Elections: How Data-Driven Election Monitoring Can Improve Our Democracy.* Cambridge, UK: Cambridge University Press.

Ananda, A. and Bol, D., 2021. "Does Knowing Democracy Affect Answers to Democratic Support Questions? A Survey Experiment in Indonesia." *International Journal of Public Opinion Research* 33(2): 433–443.

Anderson, C. J. and Guillory, C. A., 1997. "Political Institutions and Satisfaction with Democracy: A Cross-National Analysis of Consensus and Majoritarian Systems." *American Political Science Review* 91(1): 66–81.

Anderson, C. J. and LoTempio, A. J., 2002. "Winning, Losing and Political Trust in America." *British Journal of Political Science* 32(2): 335–351.

Anderson, C. J. and Mendes, S., 2005. "Learning to Lose: Election Outcomes, Democratic Experience and Political Protest Potential." *British Journal of Political Science* 36(1): 91–111.

Anderson, C. J. and Tverdova, Y. V., 2003. "Corruption, Political Allegiances, and Attitudes towards Government in Contemporary Democracies." *American Journal of Political Science* 47(1): 91–109.

Anderson, C. J., Bol, D., and Ananda, A., 2021. "Humanity's Attitudes about Democracy and Political Leaders: Patterns and Trends." *Public Opinion Quarterly* 85(4): 957–986.

Anderson, C. J., Blais, A., Bowler, S., Donovan, T., and Listhaug, O., 2005. *Loser's Consent and Democratic Legitimacy.* Oxford: Oxford University Press.

Apolte, T. 2018. "A Theory of Autocratic Transition. Prerequisites to Self-Enforcing Democracy," Beiträge zur Jahrestagung des Vereins für Socialpolitik 2018: Digitale Wirtschaft – Session: Institutions, No. A17-V1, ZBW – Leibniz-Informationszentrum Wirtschaft, Kiel, Hamburg.

Ariely, G., 2015. "Democracy-Assessment in Cross-National Surveys: A Critical Examination of How People Evaluate Their Regime." *Social Indicators Research* 121(3): 621–635.

Armingeon, K. and Guthman, K., 2014. "Democracy in Crisis? The Declining Support in European Countries, 2007–2011." *European Journal of Political Research* 53(3): 423–442.

Beaulieu, E. and Hyde, S. D., 2009. "In the Shadow of Democracy Promotion: Strategic Manipulation, International Observers, and Election Boycotts." *Comparative Political Studies* 42(3): 392–415.

Bélanger, E. and Aarts. K., 2006. "Explaining the Rise of the LPF: Issues, Discontent, and the 2002 Dutch Election." *Acta Politica* 41(1): 4–20.

Bernauer, J. and Vatter, A., 2011. "Consensus Democracy Indicators in 35 Democracies, 1997–2006." *Berne/Konstanz: Department of Political Science*.

Bernauer, J. and Vatter, A., 2012. "Can't Get No Satisfaction with the Westminster Model? Winners, Losers and the Effects of Consensual and Direct Democratic Institutions on Satisfaction with Democracy." *European Journal of Political Research* 51(4): 435–468.

Best, R. E. and Seyis, D., 2021. "How Do Voters Perceive Ideological Congruence? The Effects of Winning and Losing under Different Electoral Rules." *Electoral Studies* 69: 102201.

Birch, S., 2008. "Electoral Institutions and Popular Confidence in Electoral Process: A Cross-National Analysis." *Electoral Studies* 27(2): 305–320.

Birch, S., 2011. *Electoral Malpractice*. Oxford: Oxford University Press.

Blais, A. and Daoust, J.-F., 2020. *The Motivation to Vote: Explaining Electoral Participation*. Vancouver: University of British Columbia Press.

Blais, A. and Daoust, J.-F., 2021. "A Better Way to Hold Leaders' Debates in Elections." *Policy Options*. https://policyoptions.irpp.org/magazines/october-2021/a-better-way-to-hold-leaders-debates-in-elections/.

Blais, A. and Gélineau, F., 2007. "Winning, Losing and Satisfaction with Democracy." *Political Studies* 55(2): 425–441.

Blais, A., Bol, D., Bowler, S. et al. 2021. "What Kind of Electoral Outcome do People Think is Good for Democracy?" *Political Studies*, 00323217211055560.

Bol, D., Blais, A., Gillard, X., Lopez, L. N., and Pilet, J. B., 2018. "Voting and Satisfaction with Democracy in Flexible List PR." *Electoral Studies* 56: 23–34.

Bol, D., Giani, M., Blais, A., and Loewen, P. J., 2021. "The Effect of COVID-19 Lockdowns on Political Support: Some Good News for Democracy?" *European Journal of Political Research* 60(2): 497–505.

Borman, N.-C. and Golder, M., 2013. "Democratic Electoral Systems around the World, 1946–2011." *Electoral Studies* 32(2): 360–369.

Bormann, N.-C. and Golder, M., 2013. "Democratic Electoral Systems around the World, 1946–2011" *Electoral Studies* 32(2): 360–369.

Bowler, S., 2016. "I Study Democracies, and What I've Learned Is This: They Collapse without Graceful Losers." *The Big Idea*. October 14. www.vox .com/the-big-idea/2016/10/14/13277626/losers-democratic-transition-san ders-trump.

Bowler, S., Brunell, T., Donovan, T., and Gronke, P., 2015. "Election Administration and Perceptions of Fair Elections." *Electoral Studies* 38(1): 1–9.

Bratton, M. and Mattes, R., 2001. "Support for Democracy in Africa: Intrinsic or Instrumental?" *British Journal of Political Science* 31(3): 447–474.

Brody-Barre, A. G., 2013. "The Impact of Political Parties and Coalition Building on Tunisia's Democratic Future." *The Journal of North African Studies* 18(2): 211–230.

Canache, D., Mondak, J. J., and Seligson, M. A., 2001. "Meaning and Measurement in Cross-National Research on Satisfaction with Democracy." *Public Opinion Quarterly* 65(4): 506–528.

Cantu, F. and Garcia-Ponce, O., 2015. "Partisan Losers' Effects: Perceptions of Electoral Integrity in Mexico." *Electoral Studies* 39(1): 1–14.

Carey, J. M., Helmke, G., Nyhan, B. et al. 2021. "The Effect of Electoral Inversions on Democratic Legitimacy: Evidence from the United States." *British Journal of Political Science* 52(4): 1–11.

Carreras, M. and Irepoglu, Y., 2013. "Trust in Elections, Vote Buying and Turnout in Latin America." *Electoral Studies* 32(4): 609–619.

Cervas, J. R. and Grofman, B., 2019. "Are Presidential Inversions Inevitable? Comparing Eight Counterfactual Rules for Electing the US President." *Social Science Quarterly* 100(4): 1322–1342.

Chernykh, S. and Slovik, M. W., 2015. "Third-Party Actors and the Success of Democracy: How Election Commissions, Courts and Observers Shape Incentives for Electoral Manipulation and Post-Electoral Protests." *Journal of Politics* 77(2): 407–420.

Chong, D. and Druckman, J. N., 2007. "Framing Theory." *Annual Review of Political Science* 10: 103–126.

Christmann, P., 2018. "Economic Performance, Quality of Democracy and Satisfaction with Democracy." *Electoral Studies* 53(1): 79–89.

Citrin, J., Levy, M., and Wright, M., 2014. "Multicultural Policy and Political Support in European Democracies." *Comparative Political Studies* 47(11): 1531–1557.

Claasen, C., 2020. "Does Public Support Help Democracy Survive?" *American Journal of Political Science* 64(1): 118–134.

Coppedge, M., Gerring, J., Knutsen, C. H. et al. 2018. "V-Dem [Country-Year/Country-Date] Dataset v8. Varieties of Democracy (V-Dem) Project."

Cordero, G. and Simón, P., 2016. "Economic Crisis and Support for Democracy in Europe." *West European Politics* 39(2): 305–325.

Curini, L., Jou, W., and Memoli. V., 2012. "Satisfaction with Democracy and the Winner/Loser Debate: The Role of Policy Preferences and Past Experience." *British Journal of Political Science* 42(2): 241–261.

Dahl, R., 1971. *Polyarchy: Participation and Opposition.* Yale: Yale University Press.

Dahl, R., 1989. *Democracy and its Critics.* New Haven: Yale University Press.

Dahl, R., 1998. *On Democracy.* New Haven: Yale University Press.

Dahlberg, S. and Linde, J., 2016. "Losing Happily? The Mitigating Effect of Democracy and Quality of Government on the Winner–Loser Gap in Political Support." *International Journal of Public Administration* 39(9): 652–664.

Dahlberg, S., Linde, J., and Holmberg, S., 2015. "Democratic Discontent in Old and New Democracies: Assessing the Importance of Democratic Input and Governmental Output." *Political Studies* 63(S1): 18–37.

Dalton, R. J., 2004. *Democratic Challenges, Democratic Choices.* Oxford, UK: Oxford University Press.

Dalton, R. J. and Welzel, C., 2014. *The Civic Culture Transformed: From Allegiant to Assertive Citizens.* New York: Cambridge University Press.

Dalton, R. J., Sin, T., and Chou, W., 2007. "Understanding Democracy: Data from Unlikely Places" *Journal of Democracy* 18(2): 142–156.

Daoust, J.-F. and Blais, A., 2017. "How Much Do Voters Care about the Electoral Outcome in Their District?" *Representation* 53(3–4): 233–246.

Daoust, J.-F. and Blais, A., 2021. "Electoral Behaviour in Multilevel Systems." In Lago, I. (ed), *Handbook on Decentralization, Devolution and the State.* Cheltenham: Edward Elgar Publishing, pp. 255–268.

Daoust, J.-F., and Nadeau, R., 2021. "Context Matters: Economics, Politics and Satisfaction with Democracy." *Electoral Studies* 74: 102133.

Daoust, J.-F., Blais, A., and Péloquin-Skulski, G., 2021. "What Do Voters Do When They Prefer a Leader from Another Party?" *Party Politics* 27(2): 308–316.

Daoust, J.-F., Plescia, C., and Blais, A., 2023. "Are People More Satisfied with Democracy When They Feel They Won the Election? No." *Political Studies Review* 21(1): 162–171.

Daoust, J.-F., Ridge, H. M., and Mongrain, P., 2023. "Electoral Outcomes and Satisfaction with Democracy: A Comparison of Regional and National Elections." *Electoral Studies* 84: 102642.

Dassonneville, R. and Hooghe, M., 2017. "The Noise of the Vote Recall Question: The Validity of the Vote Recall Question in Panel Studies in Belgium, Germany, and the Netherlands." *International Journal of Public Opinion Research* 29(2): 316–338.

Dassonneville, R. and McAllister, I., 2020. "The Party Choice Set and Satisfaction with Democracy." *West European Politics* 43(1): 49–73.

Dassonneville, R., Blais, A., Hooghe, M., and Deschouwer, K., 2020. "The Effects of Survey Mode and Sampling in Belgian Election Studies: A Comparison of a National Probability Face-to-Face Survey and a Nonprobability Internet Survey." *Acta Politica* 55(2): 175–198.

Dassonneville, R., Blais, A., Sevi, S., and Daoust, J.-F., 2021. "How Citizens Want Their Legislator to Vote." *Legislative Studies Quarterly* 46(2): 297–321.

Davis, D. W., 2000. "Individual Level Examination of Postmaterialism in the US: Political Tolerance, Racial Attitudes, Environmentalism, and Participatory Norms." *Political Research Quarterly* 53(3): 455–475.

Daxecker, U. and Fjelde, H., 2022. "Electoral Violence, Partisan Identity, and Perceptions of Election Quality: A Survey Experiment in West Bengal, India." *Comparative Politics* 55(1): 47–69.

Daxecker, U. and Schneider, G., 2014. "Electoral Observers: The Implications of Multiple Monitors for Electoral Integrity." In Norris, P., Frank, R. W., and Martinez I Coma, F. (eds), *Advancing Electoral Integrity*. New York: Oxford University Press, pp. 73–93.

Daxecker, U., Amicarelli, E., and Jung, A., 2019. "Electoral Contention and Violence (ECAV): A New Dataset." *Journal of Peace Research* 56(5): 714–723.

Dennis, J., 1970. "Support for the Institution of Elections in the Mass Public." *American Political Science Review* 64(3): 819–836.

Dennison, J., 2019. "A Review of Public Issues Salience: Concepts, Determinants and Effects on Voting." *Political Studies Review* 17(4): 436–46.

Donovan, T. and Karp, J., 2017. "Electoral Rules, Corruption, Inequality and Evaluations of Democracy." *European Journal of Political Research* 56(3): 469–486.

Easton, D., 1965. *A Framework for Political Analysis*. Englewood Cliffs: Prentice-Hall.

Easton, D., 1975. "A Re-assessment of the Concept of Political Support." *British Journal of Political Science* 5(4): 435–457.

Enders, A. M. and Thornton, J. R., 2021. "Racial Resentment, Electoral Loss, and Satisfaction with Democracy among Whites in the United States: 2004–2016." *Political Behavior* 44(1): 1–22.

Estlund, D., 2007. "On Following Orders in an Unjust War." *Journal of Political Philosophy* 15(2): 213–34.

Evans, G. and Whitefield, S., 1995. "The Politics and Economics of Democratic Commitment: Support for Democracy in Transition Societies." *British Journal of Political Science* 25(3): 485–514.

Farrell, D. M., and McAllister, I. 2006. "Voter Satisfaction and Electoral Systems: Does Preferential Voting in Candidate-Centred Systems Make a Difference?" *European Journal of Political Research* 45(5): 723–749.

Fauvet, J., 1964. *Histoire du Parti communiste français.* Paris: Fayard.

Fearon, J. D., 2011. "Self-Enforcing Democracy." *Quarterly Journal of Economics* 126(4): 1661–1708.

Felsenthal, D. S. and Miller, N. R., 2015. "What to Do about Election Inversions under Proportional Representation?" *Representation* 51(2): 173–186.

Ferland, B., 2015. "A Rational or a Virtuous Citizenry? – The Asymmetric Impact of Biases in Votes-Seats Translation on Citizens' Satisfaction with Democracy." *Electoral Studies* 40: 394–408.

Ferland, B., 2021. "Policy Congruence and Its Impact on Satisfaction with Democracy." *Electoral Studies* 69: 102204.

Ferrin, M., 2016. "An Empirical Assessment of Democracy." In Ferrin, M. and Kriesi, H. (eds). *How Europeans View and Evaluate Democracy.* Oxford: Oxford University Press, pp. 283–306.

Fischer, J. and Sällberg, Y., 2020. "Electoral Integrity- The Winner Takes All? Evidence from Three British Elections." *The British Journal of Politics and International Relations* 22(3): 404–420.

Foa, R. S. and Mounk, Y., 2017. "The Signs of Deconsolidation." *Journal of Democracy* 28(1): 5–15.

Foa, R.S., Klassen, A., Slade, M., Rand, A. and R. Williams., 2020. *The Global Satisfaction with Democracy Report 2020.* Cambridge, UK: Centre for the Future of Democracy.

Fortin-Rittberger, J., Harfst, P., and Dingler, S. C., 2017. "The Costs of Electoral Fraud: Establishing the Link between Electoral Integrity, Winning an Election, and Satisfaction with Democracy." *Journal of Elections, Public Opinion and Parties* 27(3): 350–368.

Gafuri, A., 2021. "Can Democracy Aid Improve Democracy? The European Union's Democracy Assistance 2002–2018." *Democratization* 29(5): 777–97.

Gallet, L., 2015. "Le FN, premier parti de France? Une question dépassée." *L'Express*, août 2015.

Garnett, H. A., 2019. "On the Front Lines of Democracy: Perceptions of Officials and Democratic Elections." *Democratization* 26(8): 1399–1418.

Gattermann, K., Meyer, T. M., and Wurzer, K. 2021. "Who Won the Election? Explaining News Coverage of Election Results in Multi-Party Systems." *European Journal of Political Research* 61(4): 857–77.

Gehlbach, S. and Sonin, K., 2014. "Government Control of the Media." *Journal of Public Economics* 118: 163–171.

Gelman, A. and Hill, J., 2006. *Data Analysis Using Regression and Multilevel/ Hierarchical Models*. Cambridge: Cambridge University Press.

Geruso, M., Spears, D., and Talesara, I., 2022. "Inversions in US Presidential Elections: 1836–2016." *American Economic Journal: Applied Economics* 14(1): 327–357.

Ginsberg, B. and Weissberg, R., 1978. "Elections and the Mobilization of Popular Support." *American Journal of Political Science* 22(1): 31–55.

Ginsberg, B., 1982. *The Consequences of Consent: Elections, Citizen Control and Popular Acquiescence*. Reading: Addison-Wesley.

Golder, S. N., Lago, I., Blais, A., Gidengil, E., and Gschwend, T., 2017. *Multi-level Electoral Politics: Beyond the Second-Order Election Model*. Oxford: Oxford University Press.

Greene, W. H., 2012. *Econometric Analysis* (7th ed.). Upper Saddle River: Prentice Hall.

Halliez, A. A. and Thornton, J. R., 2022. "The Winner-Loser Satisfaction Gap in the Absence of a Clear Outcome." *Party Politics* 29(2): 260–69.

Han, S. M., and Chang, E. C., 2016. "Economic Inequality, Winner-Loser Gap, and Satisfaction with Democracy." *Electoral Studies* 44(1): 85–97.

Hansen, M. A. and Olsen, J., 2019. "Flesh of the Same Flesh: A Study of Voters for the Alternative for Germany (AfD) in the 2017 Federal Election." *German Politics* 28(1): 1–19.

Harteveld, E., 2021. "Fragmented Foes: Affective Polarization in the Multiparty Context of the Netherlands." *Electoral Studies* 71: 102332.

Harteveld, E., Kokkonen, A., Linde, J., and Dahlberg, S., 2021. "A Tough Trade-off? The Asymmetrical Impact of Populist Radical Right Inclusion on Satisfaction with Democracy and Government." *European Political Science Review* 13(1): 113–133.

Hellwig, T., Kweon, Y., and Vowles, J., 2020. *Democracy under Siege? Parties, Voters, and Elections after the Great Recession*. Oxford, UK: Oxford University Press.

Hooghe, M. and Dassonneville, R., 2018. "A Spiral of Distrust: A Panel Study on the Relation between Political Distrust and Protest Voting in Belgium." *Government and Opposition* 53(1): 104–130.

Hooghe, M. and Stiers, D., 2016. "Elections as a Democratic Linkage Mechanism: How Elections Boost Political Trust in a Proportional System." *Electoral Studies* 44: 46–55.

Huang, M.-h., Chang, Y.-t., and Chu, Y.-h., 2008. "Identifying Sources of Democratic Legitimacy: A Multilevel Analysis." *Electoral Studies* 27(1): 45–62.

Hyde, S. and Marinov, N., 2012. "Which Elections Can Be Lost?" *Political Analysis* 20(2): 191–210.

Hyde, S. D. and Marinov, N., 2014. "Information and Self-Enforcing Democracy: The Role of International Observation." *International Organization* 68(2): 329–359.

Hyde, S. D. and Marinov, N., 2019. *Codebook for National Elections across Democracy and Autocracy Dataset, 5.0.* http://nelda.co.

Inglehart, R., 1999. "Postmodernization Brings Declining Respect for Authority but Rising Support for Democracy." In Norris, P. (ed). *Critical Citizens: Global Support for Democratic Government.* Oxford: Oxford University Press, pp. 236–56.

Jungkunz, S., Fahey, R. A., and Hino, A., 2021. "How Populist Attitudes Scales Fail to Capture Support for Populists in Power." *PLoS One* 16(12): e0261658.

Kaniovski, S. and Zaigraev, A., 2018. "The Probability of Majority Inversion in a Two-Stage Voting System with Three States." *Theory and Decision* 84(4): 525–546.

Karp, J. A. and Banducci, S. A., 2008. "Political Efficacy and Participation in Twenty–Seven Democracies: How Electoral Systems Shape Political Behaviour." *British Journal of Political Science* 38(2): 311–334.

Karp, J. A., Nai, A., and Norris, P. 2018. "Dial 'F' for Fraud: Explaining Citizens Suspicions about Elections." *Electoral Studies* 53: 11–19.

Keefer, P., 2007. "Clientelism, Credibility, and the Policy Choices of Young Democracies." *American Journal of Political Science* 51(3): 804–821.

Kernell, G. and Mullinix, K. J., 2019. "Winners, Losers, and Perceptions of Vote (mis) Counting." *International Journal of Public Opinion Research* 31(1): 1–24.

Kittilson, M. C. and Anderson, C. J., 2011. "Electoral Supply and Voter Turnout." In Dalton, R. J. and Anderson, C. J. (eds). *Citizens, Context, and Choice,* Oxford: Oxford University Press, pp. 33–54.

König, P. D., Siewert, M. B., and Ackermann, K., 2022. "Conceptualizing and Measuring Citizens' Preferences for Democracy: Taking Stock of Three

Decades of Research in a Fragmented Filed." *Comparative Political Studies,* 55(12): 2015–49.

Kornberg, A. and Clarke, H. D., 1994. "Beliefs about Democracy and Satisfaction with Democratic Government: The Canadian Case." *Political Research Quarterly* 47(3): 537–563.

Kostelka, F. and Blais. A., 2018. "The Chicken and Egg Question: Satisfaction with Democracy and Voter Turnout." *Political Science & Politics* 51(2): 370–376.

Krieckhaus, J., Son, B., Bellinger, N. M., and Wells, J. M., 2014. "Economic Inequality and Democratic Support." *The Journal of Politics* 76(1): 139–51.

Kunda, Z., 1990. "The Case for Motivated Reasoning." *Psychological Bulletin* 108(3): 480–98.

Kurrild-Klitgaard, P., 2013. "Election Inversions, Coalitions and Proportional Representation: Examples of Voting Paradoxes in Danish Government Formations." *Scandinavian Political Studies* 36(2): 121–136.

Lago, I. (Ed.). 2021. *Handbook on Decentralization, Devolution and the State.* Cheltenham: Edward Elgar Publishing.

Layard, R., Mayraz, G., and Nickell, S., 2008. "The Marginal Utility of Income." *Journal of Public Economics* 92(8): 1846–57.

Lehoucq, F., 2003. "Electoral Fraud: Causes, Types, and Consequences." *Annual Review of Political Science* 6(1): 233–256.

Lelkes, Y., 2016. "Winners, Losers, and the Press: The Relationship between Political Parallelism and the Legitimacy Gap." *Political Communication* 33(4): 523–543.

Lewis-Beck, M. S. and Stegmaier, M., 2013. "The VP-Function Revisited: A Survey of the Literature on Vote and Popularity Functions after over 40 Years." *Public Choice* 157(3): 367–385.

Lijphart, A. 1999. *Patterns of Democracy: Government Forms and Performance in Thirty-Six Countries.* New Haven: Yale University Press.

Linde, J. and Ekman, J., 2003. "Satisfaction with Democracy: A Note on a Frequently Used Indicator in Comparative Politics." *European Journal of Political Research* 42(3): 391–408.

Linz, J. J. and Stepan, A. C., 1996a. "Toward Consolidated Democracies." *Journal of Democracy* 7(2): 14–33.

Linz, J. J. and Stepan, A. C., 1996b. *Problems of Democratic Transition and Consolidation: Southern Europe, South America, and Post-Communist Europe.* Baltimore: John Hopkins University Press.

Lipset, S. M., 1959. "Some Social Requisites of Democracy: Economic Development and Political Legitimacy." *American Political Science Review* 53(1): 69–105.

Lodge, M. and Taber, C., 2000. "Three Steps toward a Theory of Motivated Political Reasoning." In Lupia, A., McCubbins, M. D., and Popkin, S. L. (eds), *Elements of Reason: Cognition, Choice, and the Bounds of Rationality.* Cambridge, UK: Cambridge University Press, pp. 183–213.

Lodge, M. and Taber, C. S., 2013. *The Rationalizing Voter.* Cambridge, UK: Cambridge University Press.

Loveless, M. and Binelli, C., 2020. "Economic Expectations and Satisfaction with Democracy: Evidence from Italy." *Government and Opposition* 55(3): 413–429.

Lühiste, K., 2014. "Social Protection and Satisfaction with Democracy: A Multi-Level Analysis." *Political Studies* 62(4): 784–803.

Luhrmann, A., Lindberg, S. I., and Tannenberg, M., 2017. "Regimes in the World (RIW): A Robust Regime Type Measure Based on V-Dem." V-Dem Working Paper No. 47.

Magalhães, P. C., 2016. "Economic Evaluations, Procedural Fairness, and Satisfaction with Democracy." *Political Research Quarterly* 69(3): 522–534.

Marien, S. and Kern, A., 2018. "The Winner Takes It All: Revisiting the Effect of Direct Democracy on Citizens' Political Support." *Political Behaviour* 40(4): 857–882.

Martini, S. and Quaranta, M., 2019. "Political Support among Winners and Losers: Within-and between-Country Effects of Structure, Process and Performance in Europe." *European Journal of Political Research* 58(1): 341–361.

Mattes, R. and Bratton, M., 2007. "Learning about Democracy in Africa: Awareness, Performance, and Experience." *American Journal of Political Science* 51(1): 192–217.

Mauk, M., 2020. "Electoral Integrity Matters: How Electoral Process Conditions the Relationship between Political Losing and Political Trust." *Quantity and Quality* 56(3): 1709–28.

McAllister, I. and Quinlan, S., 2022. "Vote Overreporting in National Election Surveys: A 55-Nation Exploratory Study." *Acta Politica* 57(3): 529–547.

McAllister, I. and White, S., 1994. "Political Participation in Post-communist Russia: Voting, Activism, and the Potential of Mass Protest." *Political Studies* 42(4): 593–615.

McAllister, I. and White, S., 2011. "Public Perceptions of Electoral Fairness in Russia." *Europe Asia Studies* 63(4): 663–683.

Miller, D. T., 2001. "Disrespect and the Experience of Injustice." *Annual Review of Psychology* 52(1): 527–553.

Miller, A. H., Hesli, V., and Reisengen, W. M., 1997. "Conceptions of Democracy among Mass and Elite in Post-Soviet Societies." *British Journal of Political Science* 27(1): 157–190.

Mochtak, M., Lesschaeve, C., and Giaurdic, J., 2021. "Voting and Winning: Perceptions of Electoral Integrity in Consolidating Democracies." *Democratization* 28(8): 1423–1441.

Moehler, D. C., 2009. "Critical Citizens and Submissive Subjects: Election Losers and Winner in Africa." *British Journal of Political Science* 39(2): 345–366.

Morin-Chassé, A., Bol, D., Stephenson, L. B., and St-Vincent, S. L., 2017. "How to Survey about Electoral Turnout? The Efficacy of the Face-Saving Response Items in 19 Different Contexts." *Political Science Research and Methods* 5(3): 575–584.

Nadeau, R. and Blais, A., 1993. "Accepting the Election Outcome: The Effect of Participation on Losers' Consent." *British Journal of Political Science* 23(4): 553–563.

Nadeau, R., Arel-Bundock, V., and Daoust, J.-F., 2019. "Satisfaction with Democracy and the American Dream." *The Journal of Politics* 81(4): 1080–1084.

Nadeau, R., Daoust, J.-F., and Dassonneville, R., 2023. "Winning, Losing, and the Quality of Democracy." *Political Studies* 71(2): 483–500.

Nadeau, R., Lewis-Beck, M. S., and Bélanger, É., 2013. "Economics and Elections Revisited." *Comparative Political Studies* 46(2): 551–573.

Nadeau, R., Blais, A., Nevitte, N., and Gidengil, E., 2000. "Elections and Satisfaction with Democracy." Paper prepared for delivery at the annual meeting of the *American Political Science Association*. Washington, DC, August 30–September 3, .

Nadeau, R., Bélanger, É., Lewis-Beck, M. S., Gélineau, F., and Turgeon, M., 2017. *Latin American Elections: Choice and Change*. Ann Arbor: University of Michigan Press.

Nannestad, P. and Paldam, M., 1994. "The VP-Function: A Survey of the Literature on Vote and Popularity Functions after 25 years." *Public Choice* 79(3): 213–245.

Newman, M., 2002. "Reconceptualising Democracy in the European Union." In Anderson, J. (ed), *Transnational Democracy: Political Spaces and Border Crossings*. London: Routledge, pp. 73–92.

Nisbet, E. C., Mortenson, C., and Li, Q., 2021. "The Presumed Influence of Election Misinformation on Others Reduces Our Own Satisfaction with Democracy." *The Harvard Kennedy School Misinformation Review* no 7.

Norris, P., 1999. *Critical Citizens: Global Support for Democratic Government.* Oxford: Oxford University Press .

Norris, P., 2011. *Democratic Deficit: Critical Citizens Revisited.* Cambridge, UK: Cambridge University Press.

Norris, P., 2013. "The New Research Agenda Studying Electoral Integrity." *Electoral Studies* 32(4): 563–575.

Norris, P., 2014. *Why Electoral Integrity Matters.* New York: Cambridge University Press.

Norris, P., 2015. *Why Elections Fail.* New York: Cambridge University Press.

Norris, P., 2017. *Strengthening Electoral Democracy.* Cambridge: Cambridge University Press.

Norris, P., 2019 "Do Perceptions of Electoral Malpractice Undermine Democratic Satisfaction?: The US in Comparative Perspective." *International Political Science Review* 40(1): 5–22.

Norris, P., Frank, R., and Martinez I Coma, F., 2014. "Measuring Electoral Integrity around the World: A New Dataset." *Political Science and Politics* 47(4): 789–798.

Norris, P., Garnett, H. A., and Grömping, M., 2020. "The Paranoid Style of American Elections: Explaining Perceptions of Electoral Integrity in an Age of Populism." *Journal of Elections, Public Opinion and Parties* 30(1): 105–125.

Oesch, D., 2008. "Explaining Workers' Support for Right-Wing Populist Parties in Western Europe: Evidence from Austria, Belgium, France, Norway, and Switzerland." *International Political Science Review* 29(3): 349–373.

Otjes, S. and Stiers, D., 2021. "Accountability and Alternation. How Wholesale and Partial Alternation Condition Retrospective Voting." *Party Politics* 28(3): 457–67.

Pfeifer, C. and Schneck, S., 2017. "Do Unfair Perceived Own Pay and Top Managers' Pay Erode Satisfaction with Democracy?" *Applied Economics Letters* 24(17): 1263–1266.

Plescia, C., 2019. "On the Subjectivity of the Experience of Victory: Who are the Election Winners?" *Political Psychology* 40(4): 797–814.

Plescia, C., Blais, A., and Högström, J., 2020. "Do People Want a 'Fairer' Electoral System? An Experimental Study in Four Countries." *European Journal of Political Research* 59(4): 733–751.

Plescia, C., Daoust, J.-F., and Blais, A., 2021. "Do European Elections Enhance Satisfaction with European Union Democracy?" *European Union Politics* 22(1): 94–113.

Politico. 2022. "OSCE Recommends Full-Scale Electoral Monitoring Mission in Hungary." February 5. www.politico.eu/article/osce-recommends-full-scale-election-mission-in-hungary-viktor-orban/

Powell Jr, G. B., 2004. "The Quality of Democracy: The Chain of Responsiveness." *Journal of Democracy* 15(4): 91–105.

Przeworski, A., 1991. *Democracy and the Market: Political and Economic Reforms in Eastern Europe and Latin America*. New York: Cambridge University Press.

Przeworski, A., 2005. "Democracy as an Equilibrium." *Public Choice* 123(3–4): 253–273.

Przeworski, A., 2008. "The Poor and the Viability of Democracy." In Krishna, A. (ed), *Poverty, Participation and Democracy: A Global Perspective*. New York: Cambridge University Press, pp. 125–147.

Quaranta, M., and Martini, S., 2016. "Does the Economy Really Matter for Satisfaction with Democracy? Longitudinal and Cross-country Evidence from the European Union." *Electoral Studies* 42: 164–174.

Quaranta, M. and Martini, S., 2017. "Easy Come, Easy Go? Economic Performance and Satisfaction with Democracy in Southern Europe in the Last Three Decades." *Social Indicators Research* 131(2): 659–80.

Quaranta, M., Cancela, J., Martín, I., and Tsirbas, Y., 2021. "Trust, Satisfaction and Political Engagement during Economic Crisis: Young Citizens in Southern Europe." *South European Society and Politics* 26(2): 153–79.

Radcliff, B., 2001. "Politics, Markets, and Life Satisfaction: The Political Economy of Human Happiness." *The American Political Science Review* 95(4): 939–952.

Redlawsk, D. P., Civettini, A. J. W., and Emmerson, K. M., 2010. "The Affective Tipping Point: Do Motivated Reasoners Ever 'Get It'?" *Political Psychology* 31(4): 563–593.

Reher, S., 2015. "Explaining Cross-National Variation in the Relationship between Priority Congruence and Satisfaction with Democracy." *European Journal of Political Research* 54(1): 160–181.

Repucci, S., 2019. *Media Freedom: A Downward Spiral*. Freedom House: Freedom and the Media 2019. freedomhouse.org/report/freedom-and-media/media-freedom-downward-spiral.

Ridge, H. M., 2022. "Electoral Outcomes and Support for Westminster Democracy." *Journal of Elections, Public Opinion and Parties* 32(4): 887–906.

Rogowski, R., 1974. *Rational Legitimacy*. Princeton: Princeton University Press.

Rohrschneider, R. and Loveless, M., 2010. "Macro Salience: How Economic and Political Contexts Mediate Popular Evaluations of the Democracy Deficit in the European Union." *The Journal of Politics* 72(4): 1029–1045.

Rooduijn, M., Van Der Brug, W., and De Lange, S. L., 2016. "Expressing or Fuelling Discontent? The Relationship between Populist Voting and Political Discontent." *Electoral Studies* 43: 32–40.

Saïkkonen, I.-L. and White, A. C., 2021. "Strategic Targeting: Authoritarian Capacity, State Dependent Populations, and Electoral Manipulation." *Journal of Elections, Public Opinion and Parties* 31(2): 159–179.

Schattschneider, E. E., 1960. *The Semisovereign People: A Realist's View of Democracy in America*. New York: Holt, Reinhart, and Winston.

Schakel, A. H. and Romanova, V., 2018. "Towards a Scholarship on Regional Elections." *Regional & Federal Studies* 28(3): 233–252.

Schedler, A., 2013. *The Politics of Uncertainty: Sustaining and Subverting Electoral Authoritarianism*. Oxford: Oxford University Press.

Schedler, A., 2002a. "The Nested Game of Democratization by Elections." *International Political Science Review* 23(1): 103–122.

Schedler, A., 2002b. "The Menu of Manipulation." *Journal of Democracy* 13(2): 36–50.

Selb, P. and Munzert, S., 2013. "Voter Overrepresentation, Vote Misreporting, and Turnout Bias in Postelection Surveys." *Electoral Studies* 32(1): 186–196.

Sen, A., 1999. *Development as Freedom*. Oxford, UK: Oxford University Press.

Simpser, A., 2013. *Why Governments and Parties Manipulate Elections: Theory, Practice and Implications*. New York: Oxford University Press.

Singer, P., 1973. *Democracy and Disobedience*. New York: Clarendon Press.

Singh, S. P., 2018. "Compulsory Voting and Dissatisfaction with Democracy." *British Journal of Political Science* 48(3): 843–854.

Singh, S. P. and Mayne, Q., 2023. "Satisfaction with Democracy: A Review of a Major Public Opinion Indicator." *Public Opinion Quarterly* 87(1): 187–218.

Singh, S., Karakoç, E., and Blais, A., 2012. "Differentiating Winners: How Elections Affect Satisfaction with Democracy." *Electoral Studies* 31(1): 201–211.

Singh, S., Lago, I., and Blais, A., 2011. "Winning and Competitiveness as Determinants of Political Support." *Social Science Quarterly* 92(3): 695–709.

Skovoroda, R. and Lankina, T., 2017. "Fabricating Votes for Putin: New Tests of Fraud and Electoral Manipulation from Russia." *Post-Soviet Affairs* 33(2): 100–123.

Solt, F., 2019. "The Standardized World Income Inequality Database, Versions 8–9," https://doi.org/10.7910/DVN/LM4OWF, Harvard Dataverse, V7.

Stiers, D., Daoust, J.-F., and Blais, A., 2018. "What Makes People Believe That Their Party Won the Election?" *Electoral Studies* 55: 21–29.

Stiers, D., Hooghe, M., and Dassonneville, R., 2020. "Voting at 16: Does Lowering the Voting Age Lead to More Political Engagement? Evidence from a Quasi-Experiment in the City of Ghent (Belgium)." *Political Science Research and Methods* 9(4): 849–56.

Stockman, D., 2012. *Media Commercialisation and Authoritarianism in China.* Cambridge: Cambridge University Press.

Taylor, S. E. and Brown, J. D., 1994. "Positive Illusions and Well-Being Revisited: Separating Fact from Fiction." *Psychological Bulletin* 116(1): 21–27.

Torcal, M., 2014. "The Decline of Political Trust in Spain and Portugal: Economic Performance or Political Responsiveness?" *American Behavioral Scientist* 58(12): 1542–1567.

The Comparative Study of Electoral Systems (CSES). 2015a. CSES Module 1 Full Release (Dataset, 2015 Version). Ann Arbor: CSES.

The Comparative Study of Electoral Systems (CSES). 2015b. CSES Module 2 Full Release (Dataset, 2015 Version). Ann Arbor: CSES.

The Comparative Study of Electoral Systems (CSES). 2015c. CSES Module 3 Full Release (Dataset, 2015 Version). Ann Arbor: CSES.

The Comparative Study of Electoral Systems (CSES). 2018. CSES Module 4 Full Release (Dataset and Documentation, 2018 Version). Ann Arbor: CSES.

The Comparative Study of Electoral Systems (CSES). 2021. CSES Module 5 Third Advance Release (Dataset and Documentation, 2021 Version). https://doi.org/10.7804/cses.module5.2021-07-20, www.cses.org.

Valgarðsson, V. O. and Devine, D., 2021. "What Satisfaction with Democracy? A Global Analysis of 'Satisfaction with Democracy' Measures." *Political Research Quarterly* 75(3): 576–90.

Van Ham, C., 2014. "Getting Election Right: Measuring Electoral Integrity." *Democratization* 22(4): 714–737.

Van Ham, C., Thomassen, J., Arts, K., and Andeweg, R., 2017. *Myths and Reality of the Legitimacy Crisis.* Oxford: Oxford University Press.

Vidal, X. M., 2018. "Immigration Politics in the 2016 Election." *Political Science & Politics* 51(2): 304–8.

Wagner, A. F., Schneider, F., and Martin, H., 2009. "The Quality of Institutions and Satisfaction with Democracy in Western Europe." *European Journal of Political Research* 25(1): 30–41.

Waldron, J., 1999. "Deliberation, Disagreement, and Voting." In Slye, R. C. (ed), *Deliberative Democracy and Human Rights*. New Haven: Yale University Press, pp. 210–226.

Werner, A., 2019. "Voters' Preferences for Party Representation: Promise-Keeping, Responsiveness to Public Opinion or Enacting the Common Good." *International Political Science Review* 40(4): 486–501.

Werner, H. and Marien, S., 2022. "Process vs. Outcome? How to Evaluate the Effects of Participatory Processes on Legitimacy Perceptions." *British Journal of Political Science* 52(1): 429–436.

Whiteley, P., Clarke, H. D., Sanders, D., and Stewart, M., 2016. "Why Do Voters Lose Trust in Governments? Public Perceptions of Government Honesty and Trustworthiness in Britain 2000–2013." *The British Journal of Politics and International Relations* 18(1): 234–254.

World Bank. 2019. "GINI Index (World Bank Estimate) – Australia, Germany." *World Development Indicators*, The World Bank Group, https://data.world bank.org/indicator/SI.POV.GINI?locations=AU-DE (July 31, 2020).

Acknowledgments

Parts of the material in this Element were presented in conferences at the University of Vienna, University of Manchester, University of Edinburgh, and Université de Montréal. We thank the organizers for the invitations, as well as the participants for their comments and suggestions. Among others, we are thankful to Ruth Dassonneville, Vincent Arel-Bundock, André Blais, Markus Wagner, and Carolina Plescia for their helpful comments on previous drafts of the material in this Element. We would also like to highlight the scientific community and international teams who have been involved with the Comparative Study of Electoral Systems over the years. Our work, needless to say, would not have been possible without them. We would also like to thank Susan Hyde and Nikolay Marinov who have kept us updated about their dataset (National Elections Across Democracy and Autocracy) used in Section 2. Finally, we benefitted from great research assistantships from Hanne van den Broek, El Hadj Toure, and Lily Schricker, and we are thankful for their work. Any errors remain ours.

Cambridge Elements ≡

Campaigns and Elections

Series Editors

R. Michael Alvarez
California Institute of Technology

R. Michael Alvarez is Professor of Political and Computational Social Science at Caltech. His current research focuses on election administration and technology, campaigns and elections, and computational modeling.

Emily Beaulieu Bacchus
University of Kentucky

Emily Beaulieu Bacchus is Associate Professor of Political Science and Director of International Studies at the University of Kentucky. She is an expert in political institutions and contentious politics—focusing much of her work on perceptions of election fraud and electoral protests. Electoral Protest and Democracy in the Developing World was published with Cambridge University Press in 2014.

Charles Stewart III
Massachusetts Institute of Technology

Charles Stewart III is the Kenan Sahin Distinguished Professor of Political Science at MIT. His research and teaching focus on American politics, election administration, and legislative politics.

About the Series

Broadly focused, covering electoral campaigns & strategies, voting behavior, and electoral institutions, this Elements series offers the opportunity to publish work from new and emerging fields, especially those at the interface of technology, elections, and global electoral trends.

Cambridge Elements ⁼

Campaigns and Elections

Elements in the Series

Printed in the United States
by Baker & Taylor Publisher Services